BOOKISH WORDS

BOOKISH WORDS
& their surprising stories

DAVID CRYSTAL

BODLEIAN
LIBRARY
PUBLISHING

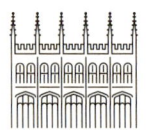

First published in 2025 by Bodleian Library Publishing
Broad Street, Oxford OX1 3BG

www.bodleianshop.co.uk

ISBN 978 1 85124 651 9

Text © David Crystal, 2025

This edition © Bodleian Library Publishing, University of Oxford, 2025

David Crystal has asserted his right to be identified
as the author of this Work.

All rights reserved.

No part of this book may be reproduced, stored in a retrieval system, or transmitted in any form or by any means, electronic, mechanical, photocopying, recording, or otherwise, without the written permission of the Bodleian Library, except for the purpose of research or private study, or criticism or review.

Publisher: Samuel Fanous
Managing Editor: Susie Foster
Editor: Janet Phillips
Picture Editor: Leanda Shrimpton
Cover design by Dot Little at the Bodleian Library
Designed and typeset by Lucy Morton of illuminati
in 10.2 on 14 New Baskerville
Printed and bound in China by C&C Offset Printing Co., Ltd.
on 120 gsm Chinese Baijin Pure paper

MIX
Paper | Supporting responsible forestry
FSC® C008047

British Library Catalogue in Publishing Data
A CIP record of this publication is available from the British Library

Contents

INTRODUCTION
1

BOOKISH WORDS
3

FURTHER READING
149

INDEX
151

Introduction

The world of books has played a notable role in the history of English vocabulary. *Book* itself is one of the oldest words in the language: *boc* in Old English (with the *o* pronounced as in *go*). It was a fruitful source of vocabulary in Anglo-Saxon times. We find such compounds as *boc-cræftig* meaning 'book-crafty' – applied to people who know their way around books, especially the Bible. And books would be found in a *boc-hord* ('book hoard') or *boca gestreon* ('book treasury'), which are to my mind much better words than the modern 'library'.

Boc meant not only 'book', as we would know it today, but any kind of written text, such as registers, catalogues, legal documents and charters. And that is the cue that has guided me in selecting the words explored in the following pages. A single word from the world of books has often generated senses and idiomatic uses that have taken it in unexpected directions, thereby increasing the lexical richness of English. With the arrival of printing, the new terminology created more opportunities for lexical growth, as did the publishing industry; and the emergence of the internet has produced still more. This book isn't an account of the specialized vocabulary of these domains, therefore, but only of those words and expressions found there that have gained a new lease of life in other settings.

The hundred or so words and idioms I've selected show these stages of influence very clearly. Each entry gives an account of the linguistic origins of a word, and for idioms an account of their original context of use. I then trace the development of their meaning over time, and conclude with examples of their current presence in everyday situations. Some unexpected and surprising contexts come to light.

I'm most grateful to Janet Phillips at Bodleian Library Publishing for suggesting that an anthology of lexical items on this theme would be interesting. So it has proved to be. In researching the different expressions, I've continually found myself travelling to linguistic places I'd not been to before. I hope others will enjoy reading about the discoveries I made on this journey.

Bookish Words

agony aunt & uncle

Agony arrived in English in the fourteenth century, a borrowing from French, and ultimately from Latin and Greek *agonia*, in the general sense of 'anguish', 'distress'; but it didn't come into the publishing world until the nineteenth century, when newspapers and magazines began to include an 'agony column', a term first recorded in 1854, though the genre can be traced back to the seventeenth century. This contained personal advertisements, such as a search for a missing person, or questions and answers about personal problems.

In American English, the journalist who responded to these questions was known as an 'advice columnist'. In Britain, over a century later, the person looking after the column came to be known as an 'agony aunt', first recorded in 1974, and a few years later an 'agony uncle'. The writers were supposedly female and male respectively, though the responses were sometimes sourced by staff writers of either gender. But some agony aunts became household names, such as the Dear Abby syndicated column in the USA and the UK's Marjorie Proops in the *Daily Mirror*. Podcasts and social media such as Instagram and TikTok have brought to the fore a new generations of advice merchants, and the family name has broadened to include 'advice (big) sisters' and '(big) brothers'. The genre has also become specialized. There are online agony aunts for gardening, singing, and probably everything. They're called 'influencers' nowadays.

anthology

Few words have developed in so many different directions at the same time as this one. It arrived in English in the early seventeenth century as part of a flood of words with classical origins. Already in the Ancient Greek period it had begun to diversify in meaning, and this diversity is seen throughout the seventeenth century. From the Hellenistic Greek period (fourth–first centuries BCE) we see its original sense, from *anthos*, meaning 'flower', 'blossom' – and so 'a collection of flowers', first recorded in 1658. But nearly forty years earlier, in 1621, we find it used in a different sense, for 'a collection of devotional pieces', especially in the Greek Orthodox Church, as seen throughout the Byzantine Greek period into medieval times. And in 1624 it comes to mean 'a published collection of short texts', such as poems or epigrams. What's the connection? In the

Greek mind, flowers symbolized the beautiful and refined sentiments that prayer and poetry express.

In English the meaning of the word steadily broadened. From 'a collection of flowers' came the notion of 'a treatise on flowers', and then – for a brief period – a technical use for their scientific study. From 'a collection of poems' came the chief modern sense: any selection of short pieces by an author, or different authors judiciously selected to represent the best of a genre, such as anthologies of Dylan Thomas, humorous verse or short stories.

In the nineteenth century it extended further, to any collection of artworks, or related items in a domain, such as ships or buildings. Then the twentieth saw it describing a musical collection, such as pop songs or their history (as in the eight-part *Beatles Anthology*, 1995). That century also saw its use in cinema, for a collection of 'short films within a film', linked by a single idea or writer, as in the 1952 production *O. Henry's Full House* – five of his short stories. Innumerable 'anthology series' appeared on radio and television, such as *The Twilight Zone* and *Walt Disney Presents*. And now, in the twenty-first century, it's in video games, such as *The Dark Picture Anthology* (2019), and on the internet, where it's used to mean a collection of... anything.

appendix

We know this word today as a description of a piece of text added to a book or document, whose content is felt to be helpful but not essential. The text is complete without it, but if you do read it, you get something extra – a 'bonus feature', as websites say these days. The word comes from the Latin verb *appendere*, meaning to 'attach' or 'add on'. The implication is clearly that an appendix appears at the end of a work. It's a surprise, then, to find that its first recorded usage refers to a piece of text at the beginning of a book.

This was in an enormous medical compendium, called *The Breviary of Health*, published by English physician Andrew Borde in 1547. He opens his text with a prologue for physicians, a prologue for surgeons, a preamble for sick or wounded men, a preface for the general reader, and then 'The apendex to all the premisses that followeth' – all 384 of them.

The word was widely used in the sixteenth century – a useful way of describing anything felt to be a subsidiary feature on the outside of an object, and its biological use for a part of the body is found soon after. The caustic Elizabethan pamphleteer Robert Greene had harsh things to say about 'upstart courtiers', obsessed with their appearance. He describes their frequent visits to the barber's shop, and gives a contemptuous account of beard-trimming options, including having 'his appendices primed [filled out], or his mustachios fostered to turn about his ears like the branches of a vine'.

Note the plural there: *appendices*. This was a reflex of the Renaissance temperament to respect classical sources, retaining Latin plural forms, even though these were highly irregular in English. *Index* and *vortex* received the same treatment. There was a period of uncertainty: if the plural was *appendices*, then surely the singular was *appendice*? But the force of analogy soon led to a regular plural form, *appendixes*. And that, in turn, brought a new period of disputed usage, with *-ices* being preferred for books and *-ixes* for bodies, and the latter slowly replacing the former in all contexts today.

back number

The term came into use in the early nineteenth century, reflecting the increased range and popularity of magazines and periodicals. Any issue other than the current one would be called a 'back number'. But by the end of the century it was being applied – at first in the United States – to persons and things. It wasn't a friendly term. To be called a 'back number' meant that you were behind the times. Any object so-called would be considered out of date. You could also use the word as a verb: to say that something had been 'back-numbered' meant that it was no longer of any use. Applied to people, it would be quite an insult.

The historical *Oxford English Dictionary* has an interesting example from 1907, illustrating how the word was coming into everyday use. In the *Westminster Gazette* we read:

> There are now so many competing forms of transport ... that the steamboat seems to be doomed to be what is in current terminology called a 'back number'.

On the other hand, not everyone thinks of the expression in such a negative way. A very successful Japanese rock power trio, formed in 2004, call themselves Back Number. But the reason for the name reflects the traditional sense. The story goes (according to the Wikipedia entry on 'Back Number') that the founder, Iyori Shimizu, chose the name because 'a girl who had dated Shimizu in high school dated another bandman. To her, Shimizu is an ex-boyfriend, a "back number". He wanted to make a "cooler" band than that guy's band with a hope that the girl might come back to him.' (Who says etymology isn't fascinating?) Complications ensued, but they didn't stop the group having a number 1 hit in Japan some years later.

bad books *see* **books: imagined**

bible

On rare occasions a book becomes so well known that its name enters everyday usage in a variety of related senses. No title matches the Judaic/Christian Bible for age and range. It came into English from French in the early Middle Ages. Before that it was in Latin, and before that in Greek, where *biblios* meant simply 'the books'. Its status as scripture, in a solidly Christian age, protected it from colloquial adaptations, but during the nineteenth century the climate changed, and *bible* came to be applied to any work viewed as authoritative.

Virtually anything could be named in this way – a cookery book, a travel guide, a publisher's style manual… Most professions today have a text its practitioners call 'The *X* Bible'. Replace the *X* by *Electrician's, Watercolour Artist's, Woodworker's,* Plumber's... Health has numerous examples: *Oral Health, Healthy Back, Arthritis...* So do animals: *Horse, Fish, Budgerigar Variety... Cat Lovers* have a *Pocket Bible. The Dog Bible* makes its status clear: 'the definitive source for all things dog'.

The first known use in this general sense was in July 1804, when poet Robert Southey wrote a letter to his friend William Taylor of Norwich – in which, incidentally, he describes Wordsworth as 'one of the wildest of all wild beasts' – and praises Taylor for something he had written, saying that it ought to be published in the *Edinburgh and Annual*, 'which bids fair to become my political bible'. *The Edinburgh Review* was an influential magazine, founded in 1802, and notorious in literary history for its critical views of the Romantic poets.

The Bible isn't the only book title to have entered everyday use. Joseph Heller's *Catch-22* will be found relating to any no-win situation. Alexander Dumas's *The Three Musketeers* for a group of three friends or associates. And a Shakespeare play title can turn up in some unexpected places An online post from an energy company in 2023 was headed: 'UK "U-turn" on net zero – or much ado about nothing?'

biro

An unusual etymology for the book world: something named after a person. This was the surname of two Hungarian brothers, László and György Bíró, who developed the technology when they were refugees in Argentina in the 1940s. They solved the problem that had caused the failure of previous attempts to produce a pen with a ball point: either the ink would run too quickly and make smudges, or it would be of the wrong consistency, clogging up the point and making smudges. Their solution was inspired by the fast-drying viscous inks used in printing.

The new pens soon became the most widely used writing implement, providing a cleaner, cheaper and more convenient alternative to dip pens and fountain pens. Originally spelled with a capital *B*, it came to be spelled with a lower-case initial, as happened to many proprietary names where the product has been successful (like *hoover* and *escalator*), and its use extended in British English to describe any ball-point pen. A verb developed: 'to biro' something – along with the annoying problem of how to spell its past tense – *biroed*, *biro'ed*, *biro'd*?

In 1950 a new design appeared, with a new name, produced by a French manufacturer of pen holders

and cases, Marcel Bich. He dropped his final letter
and named it the Bic. I was especially impressed
by this development for two linguistic reasons.
One was the way the marketing drew attention to
its potential: it would 'write for a distance of two
to three kilometres'. I can't think of a precedent
for the collocation of 'kilometres' and 'writing'.
And the other was its name: although many people
informally called it the 'bic biro', its official title was
the 'Bic Cristal'.

black book *see* **little black book**
black-letter day *see* **red-letter day**

blot one's copybook

A copybook was originally a schoolbook containing
texts, handwritten or printed, that pupils imitated
to develop their writing skills. The practice is probably as old as writing itself, but the first recorded
use of the word in English doesn't appear until
Shakespeare. He uses it in Act 5 of *Love's Labour's
Lost*, written in the mid-1590s. One of the French
ladies, Rosaline, has received a love letter from the
English lord Berowne, and the others are joking

about it. Katharine notes his initial *B*, which must have been written with a special flourish, as it reminds her of a style of formal handwriting known as 'text hand', used especially for business documents, with large letters and ornate capitals. She wryly remarks: 'Fair as a text B in a copy-book.'

Ink pens are so rarely used these days that I should (perhaps) make it clear that a blot is a stain on a piece of paper caused by too much ink being released from a pen – a quill pen, in Shakespeare's day. People at the time would complain about poor-quality pens that lost their ink in this way, or careless writers who filled their pen with too much ink. Because of its formal status and careful style, an ink blot in a document would be a disaster for a scribe. He would have to write it out all over again.

It's not surprising, then, to see the emergence of the idiom *blot one's copybook*, meaning to commit a fault that spoils a previously untarnished record or reputation, and that loses the respect of others. My favourite headline here accompanied an online article for Salford Media (27 January 2020) by reporter and historian Tony Flynn. It appears that William Cody Hickock brought his Wild West Show to Salford in 1887, which was hugely successful, and he had been applauded for his charitable work in the area. But just before he was due to leave, he had an altercation with a cab driver which led to his arrest and an appearance in court. The headline? 'The day Buffalo Bill blotted his copybook in Salford'.

blueprint

This is a nineteenth-century coinage, originally describing a photographic print showing white lines on a blue background, the colour being the result of the chemicals used in the process. The technique proved to be a fast way of reproducing architectural and other technical drawings, far more efficient and cost-effective than the previous process of having someone trace a drawing by hand. By the turn of the century, the word had broadened its meaning, referring to any plan or design that provides guidelines to achieve a particular result. People would talk about a 'blueprint for action' or a 'blueprint for healthy living'. A 1953 film noir was called *A Blueprint for Murder*.

It's proved to be one of the most appealing words for businesses and projects looking for a name. Over a thousand companies are registered with this name in the UK alone. They include such diverse subjects as community development, slot games, skateboards and marketing software. Blueprint names an event space in London, a magazine on design and architecture, a diversity award, and an album by US rapper Jay-Z. The word deserves an award itself for diversity.

Ironically, in view of this popularity, blueprints are no longer blue. Once photocopying techniques became available, and computer-aided design, drawings today are usually black on white paper, though some digital printing does silently acknowledge the tradition by using blue lines. That hasn't prevented its appeal. *Blueprint* continues to be an enticing name.

blurb

This is a short description of what a book is about, usually printed on the back cover or jacket, and often as a commendation on the front cover. 'Buy this book!', says a well-known name. As a result, it came to mean any laudatory or expository words about a product – seen on labels, tins, bottles, DVDs, posters – 'Read the blurb on the tin...' Auditory praise attracted the word too, as in television commercials and dramatically voiced film announcements. And today a website offering audio memes is called *Blerp*.

The man who invented the word was American humourist Gelett Burgess, speaking at a booksellers' annual dinner in New York in 1907. The guests had received a limited edition of his *Are You a Bromide?* (He meant someone who was dull or spoke boringly.) A special dust jacket had been printed, full of high praise, and above the title was: *YES, this is a "BLURB"*. Beneath was a picture of a woman shouting out. Her name: 'Miss Belinda Blurb … in the act of blurbing'.

The word still retains its book focus, but there have been several attempts to broaden or adapt it. An entry in the *Urban Dictionary* applies it to any short trivial piece, as in a newspaper article about something not really newsworthy. There too we find *blurbiage*, for writing that could have been more succinct – a combination of *blurb* and *verbiage*. *Blurbfuscation* describes writing that's vague and confusing. Such writing is *blurby*. But there are signs of a positive usage too. A wonderful gathering for a pride march has been called a *pride blurb*.

Were there blurbs before Burgess? Of course, but using different methods. One of the oldest was the long name. This is the title of Daniel Defoe's famous book:

> The Life And Strange Surprizing Adventures
> of Robinson Crusoe, Of York, Mariner:
> Who lived eight and twenty Years, all alone
> in an un-inhabited Island on the Coast of
> America, near the Mouth of the Great River
> of Oroonoque; Having been cast on Shore by
> Shipwreck, wherein all the Men perished but
> himself. With An Account how he was at last
> as strangely deliver'd by Pyrates.

No modern blurber could do better.

book: speaking, reading & writing

Of the four primary modes of linguistic communication – listening, speaking, reading, writing – three have generated book-related idioms. The oldest is *speak (or talk) like a book*, which has a history from the early eighteenth century, chiefly in America. It can refer to either style or content: to speak with elegance, especially using complex sentences and a literary vocabulary; or to speak with good sense about a topic in a precise and informative way.

Reading comes next, from the early nineteenth century: *to read (or know) someone like a book* is to understand that person's character and behaviour very well. They are (to use an idiom from another entry) an 'open book'. We also – though less often – find it used with plural reference: 'I can read them like books.'

Writing is the most recent, with *to write the book (on something)* known from the early twentieth century. If someone says, about some topic, they *wrote the book (on it)*, or they *could write the book (on it)*, they're claiming to be an original expert or authority on the topic or to have had more experience of it than anyone else. The topics so claimed are endless, and are usually not ones we'd expect to be a book subject. An online search brings to light dozens of examples, with people claiming to have 'written the book on' sleeplessness, vomiting, making a bad bet, missing a train… Most are negative experiences. The idiom is so common now that if someone really has written a book on a subject, they need to add a clarification: 'She's literally written a book on it.'

Which leaves listening. It's curious that there's no history for *listen to someone like an* (presumably) *audiobook*. No search results at all – yet.

bookend

This word started life in the early twentieth century as a noun – one of a pair of supports placed at each end of a row of books to stop them falling over – but by the middle of the century it was being used as a verb. If a thing or a person was 'bookended' it meant they were in the middle of two other things or happenings. The entities at each side could be physical, as when a person sits between two others, or an ornament is placed between two candles. But they could also be chronological, as when a sporting event is preceded and followed by a ceremony.

An unexpected development was when the word began to be used to refer to a *single* thing or event, positioned at just one end – usually marking the conclusion of something. A retrospective exhibition of a painter at my local arts centre was advertised as 'bookending a long career'. A conference might be bookended by a cocktail party.

It has been a popular metaphor, appearing in several specialized settings. It's used in some of the twelve-step recovery courses that cope with an addiction, such as alcohol or gambling, where it's a valuable tool to help people maintain their progress. The idea is that a person makes contact with a fellow recoverer before and after an event that might trigger the addictive behaviour, thereby avoiding a sense of isolation.

And it's used in photography. You bookend a photograph by adding visual elements on the left and right side of the frame. In a countryside scene, a person might be shown with a stone wall on each side. The idea is to give additional focus and energy to what's in the centre. Of course, the photographer could bring verb and noun together: a picture of this book, for instance, between bookends.

book of (the) words

This was originally an expression with the literal meaning of a book or booklet that contained words – that is, the words of a play or a libretto. It's recorded from the eighteenth century. George Bernard Shaw, in *How to Become a Musical Critic* (1960), remembers how, before an opera performance, in the foyer of the theatre there would be 'a gentleman who carries a bundle of white pamphlets, and cries incessantly 'Book of the words! Programme! Book of the words!' *Book* in this context became especially used in the world of twentieth-century musicals: '*Oklahoma* – music by Richard Rogers, book by Oscar Hammerstein II'.

The expression today can refer to a real book listing words, such as a dictionary or an official listing of some kind. Somebody who uses an unusual word in *Scrabble* might be challenged, and reply with 'it's in the book of words' – the official word list. But just as often the reference isn't to a book at all, which is how the phrase gained idiomatic status. In response to 'Where's the book of words?', the questioner might be passed a catalogue, a car manual, a travel brochure, an instruction leaflet, or any source that contains rules and regulations, such as *The Highway Code*. 'Let's look it up in the book' is an alternative. There may even be no words at all, as when someone asks to see a musical score, or no physical copy, as when the questioner is directed to a website.

The minimalist interpretation of the idiom is when the source is just a single page. The most bizarre instance, in my experience, was in a restaurant, where a waiter asked if I'd seen the book of words. He was referring to the menu.

books: imagined

Sometimes *book* refers to – no book. The allusion is to a totally imaginary text. When someone says 'I've tried every trick in the book, and I still can't get the thing to work', the reference is to a hypothetical book that contains all available answers. There may be no such book in existence – or, if there is, the speaker may have no idea that it exists. This idiom dates from the end of the nineteenth century. It's also used in a reduced form: *in the book*. When someone fails to perform a task efficiently, they might complain about failing to recognize (or be accused of ignoring) 'the oldest rule in the book'.

A similar usage is *in X's book*, where *X* can be a personal pronoun or a proper name. 'That was definitely a penalty, in my book', an aggrieved football supporter might say. It means 'in my opinion, in my way of seeing things'. It can be generalized, making it more emphatic: 'that was a penalty in anybody's book.' A riposte is also available: 'not in my book!' These are more recent usages, recorded since the 1930s.

Around that time, in the USA, another imaginary *book* usage developed. To say that something is 'for the book(s)' meant that it was so remarkable that it should be recorded in a book. 'That's one for the book(s)' was especially popular. It could be used

for any extraordinary event or action, and also
for a striking turn of phrase. It's since crossed the
Atlantic, and entered the most iconic British circles.
An online article lauds the Lions rugby team's 2025
tour of Austria: 'With nine incredible matches
spread over six spell-binding weeks, this tour promises to be one for the books.'

And one more: to be 'in someone's good books' –
or its opposite, '…bad books'. The meaning is clear:
to be in favour, or out of favour, with a person. It's
an old idiom, from the sixteenth century, but when
it first appeared it had no adjective. One would be
simply 'in his/her books'. Its opposite was 'out of his/
her books', a usage that died out in the following
century.

This doesn't exhaust the imaginary uses of book:
see **on/off the books** for another example.

bookworm

Insects that damage books have been around a long
time. One of them provided the solution to an Old
English verse riddle, written in the tenth-century
Exeter Book. I translate it here, keeping the original
line breaks and adding line-initial capitals and
modern punctuation:

> A moth ate words. To me that seemed
> A curious event, when I heard that wonder,
> That the worm swallowed up the song of some man,
> A thief in darkness, glorious utterance
> And its strong foundation. The thieving guest was not
> At all the wiser that he swallowed those words.

However, the actual word, *bookworm*, doesn't appear in English until the sixteenth century, and when it does it's first applied to people – those who are totally devoted to reading or, as another idiom has it, who always 'have their nose in a book'. Early uses are almost always derogatory. Playwright Ben Jonson called then 'candle-wasters'. His contemporary, writer Gabriel Harvey, paired them with heavy drinkers: 'A morning bookeworm, an afternoone maltworm' – that is, someone addicted to malt beer.

Today the word has positive associations. To call someone a bookworm usually just means that they enjoy reading a lot. Evidence of its rehabilitation, if it were needed, is to be found in modern pastimes. It's the title of a word-forming video game. And it names a character in *Toy Story 3*: an intelligent worm with a built-in flashlight, who has access to a library of instruction books for fixing toys, including the hero, Buzz Lightyear. Difficult to think of a greater accolade for a book-related word.

bring to book

Grammar raises its head in this entry. This is an idiom where the passive voice is much more common than the active. We'll hear: *The perpetrators are being brought to book* rather than [*someone*] *is bringing the perpetrators to book* – presumably because it's often not clear, relevant or known who is actually doing the bringing. The passive is the ideal grammatical construction to use when we don't want to say who or what is performing an action.

It's also an idiom used in all tense forms. We'll also hear: 'The perpetrators *will be brought* to book.' And then, hopefully: 'The perpetrators *have been brought* to book.' And again, some time later: 'The perpetrators *were brought* to book.'

The 'book' here is the same one that we find in **throw the book at someone**: a written record of crimes or punishments, viewed as a legal norm or standard. It's recorded since the late eighteenth century with the general sense of 'call to account' – either most strongly meaning 'reprimand', 'punish', or in a weaker sense of 'explain conduct', 'acknowledge wrongdoing'. It's not only used in relation to crimes, but to any behaviour thought to break the rules – in schools, clubs, sports... Nobody is exempt – including the guardians. 'Referees should be brought to book', headlined an article in the *Daily Mail* about footballers who felt refs had made too many wrong decisions.

An idiom has truly made its mark when it becomes the clue or answer in a crossword puzzle. This one often has. 'Boys brought to book (5 letters)'? Answer (if needed) on page 89.

bullets

This came in from French in the sixteenth century, where it was a diminutive form of *boule* – a *boulette* (which sounds so sweet!), meaning a small round ball, often a plaything, as in modern *boules*. It became more serious when it began to be used in weaponry: a cannonball was for a while called a 'cannon bullet'. It was a short step from there to the modern 'ball of lead' as used in firearms.

All that happened in quite a short space of time, in the 1500s. It wasn't until the 1950s that we find the first typographical use, referring to small black round dots that mark items in a list, or single out paragraphs or sections in a text for special attention. Soon after we see them called 'bullet points', and the original dot grew into a variety of shapes.

Unicode has over a dozen characters for types of bullet now: a triangular shape, one like a hyphen, an arrow, a white circle, a black circle, a floral heart, and so on.

'Bullet point' then left the publishing world behind and became a way of summarizing thoughts, issues, proposals, or anything where the speaker has a list of things in mind. 'Bullet list' became a cool alternative to 'bucket list'. And New Year resolutions? Old hat. The hip generation tells us what's on their bullet lists for the year.

by the book

It's a famous literary line. Romeo and Juliet exchange their first kiss, in Shakespeare's play, and she is somewhat taken aback: 'You kiss by th' book.' What she means is that Romeo has kissed her expertly, as if following a set of instructions in a rule book of 'how to kiss'.

The usage had only recently come into English when Shakespeare was writing. We find both *by the book* and *by book*. The latter seems to have died out now, but the former is alive and well, and also found as an adjective. A 'by-the-book solution' to a problem would be one that follows a tried or recommended approach, as opposed to one where solvers use their own initiative in unconventional, creative ways.

There may of course be a number of particular (but unnamed) books in mind. 'You can't bring a child up by the book', said a parent at a nursery family group meeting, presumably thinking of the various parenting books that exist, and affirming the value of personal decision-making. Alternatively, the 'book' may not exist at all, other than in our minds. If we describe someone as 'never doing anything by the book', we mean to draw attention to a free spirit, whose creative approach to life captures the imagination. Or, putting that another way, a refusal to conform to an indefinite number of rule books.

caption

This word came into English in the fourteenth century from a form of the Latin verb *capere* 'to take', and retained that meaning of 'taking', 'seizing', 'capturing' in its early uses. It soon came to apply to written texts, the idea being that a caption would 'capture the sense' of what the text was about. This was first seen in the opening section of a legal document introducing a case to be heard in court: the caption would give contact information about the lawyers involved, the court where the case was to be heard, the names of the parties, and so on. By the end of the eighteenth century it was being used for all kinds of headings, such as above a newspaper article or introducing a chapter in a book, and then for the short piece of text beneath an illustration, which explains what it is about. This became the dominant modern use. It transferred smoothly into cinema and television, when subtitles were introduced.

That might have been the end of the story, if social media hadn't arrived, with the opportunity being provided for people to upload their photos for everyone to see. They immediately encountered a problem: how to label them in an interesting way. Some people would be good at it, but most evidently weren't, judging by the number of online sites offering help. As one of these sites put it: 'you've snapped a cute Instagram pic and are wondering just what to say along with it.' If you want to avoid a boring or clichéd description, then these sites can provide you with text to suit your mood. Do you want to sound funny, confident, happy, inspirational…? Long lists of options are available to choose from. The texts can appear above, below or at the side of your pic. They can be short and succinct one-liners, or quite long paragraphs. And they are all called captions.

cartoon

This is a word with two lives. When it arrived in English from Italian via French in the seventeenth century it reflected its origin: *carta*, meaning 'paper', with a suffix *-one* (pronounced *oh*-nay) suggesting an increase of some kind – so, thick paper. The paper needed to be stout because it was being used in an arts setting. Artists planning a work such as a painting, fresco, tapestry or a piece of stained glass would first make a drawing of it, of roughly the same size, sometimes in colour, and this they called a cartoon. The word appears in English in the seventeenth century, and in view of its later development it takes a moment for people today to interpret such sentences as 'the set of cartoons for the tapestries of the Sistine Chapel'.

The second life didn't take place until the nineteenth century, and it was all due to a single journal, the satirical *Punch* magazine, which published its first issue in 1841. At the very end of its fourth volume, in June 1843, we read:

> *Punch* has the benevolence to announce, that in an early number of his ensuing Volume he will astonish the Parliamentary Committee by the publication of several exquisite designs, to be called Punch's Cartoons!

Then, a month later, we see 'Cartoon No. 1', a full-page drawing headed 'Substance and Shadow', showing a group of poor people in an art gallery, standing by pictures of rich people. The cartoons were all originally full-page illustrations, and they were always a comment on current affairs. But by the end of the century they had become drawings of any size, and their subject matter had broadened to include characters and situations that were humorous in their own right, not necessarily related to political issues. The 1860s saw the first comic strips, and soon after the cartoon pages in Sunday newspapers and the adjectival use of the word, as in a 'cartoon character'. The new century brought the animated cartoon of early films. We have entered the world of Mickey Mouse, Peanuts, Garfield, and uncountable others.

case *see* **out of sorts**

catchword

This must be one of the tiniest features from the world of printing to motivate an everyday lexical use. It was a really clever idea, in the age of printing by hand (from the fifteenth century to around 1800), solving the problem of how to ensure that the pages of a book would be bound together in the right order. The printers took over a convention used by scribes in their manuscripts; the first word of a page of text to be printed was also printed in the bottom right-hand corner of the preceding page, underneath the body of the text. It was called the *catchword*, often hyphenated or spaced.

It came into use at the beginning of the 1600s, and by the end of the century it had developed a general meaning: a word associated with a particular group, or which had become fashionable. In the mid-twentieth century, catchwords would also be called *buzzwords*. But the old word is still in use, though not so much among young people, who tend to think of these things as memes.

Catchword itself became a catchword in the early 1990s in the UK, when it named a popular afternoon television game show. It also (in the 1950s) named a board game where players spell out words using letters represented on cards (for consonants) and dice (for vowels).

It's not only single words that 'catch on'. During the nineteenth century, especially when comedy and novelty acts became part of music-hall programmes, catchphrases used by individual entertainers were all the rage, to be replaced eventually by stock phrases used by film characters, and later in television game shows and sitcoms. They were also a central feature of the growing world of advertising. And today the most widely known catchphrases in a country come from those domains. They don't travel internationally, apart from those where the films or adverts have a global distribution. They might then be adapted to suit occasions. May the force be with me.

chapter and verse

The verbs that usually accompany this expression are *give* and *cite*. 'I can give you chapter and verse for that', someone might say, indicating that they know an authoritative source for what they've just said. The connotations are accuracy, precision, thoroughness and specificity, even to the point – if required – of looking up the source and reading it out. Both words are from Latin: from *capitulum* 'little head' and *versus* 'a line of writing'.

The reference, of course, is to the text of the Jewish/Christian Bible, at a time when this work was considered to provide the answers to virtually any question about life and living that might be asked. The early versions had no such divisions, but the demand for a convenient means of identifying where particular passages occurred led, first, to chapter divisions in the thirteenth century, then verse divisions in the sixteenth. Both are found in the Geneva Bible of 1560 – incidentally, thought to be the one used by Shakespeare – and by the early seventeenth century the phrase 'chapter and verse' was being routinely used, both for references to the Bible and in the more general sense.

There's a certain irony in the fact that not all editions agree on the numbering, most famously in the book of Psalms, depending on which translation is used. For example, 'The Lord is my shepherd' is either Psalm 23 (in a Hebrew-based text) or Psalm 22 (in a Greek-based text) because the former treats Psalms 9 and 10 as separate, whereas the latter combines them.

But this hasn't stopped the expression achieving widespread use in everyday speech, and its succinctness and rhythmical balance have given it an appeal that has probably attracted more diverse uses than any other entry in this book. What does chapter and verse name? A five-minute online search brought to light several advice and counselling agencies; a wedding film company; a British band, a 2016 album by Bruce Springsteen and the pseudonym of a British DJ; two biographies; an American furniture-making company; adjacent office properties in Central London (Chapter House and Verse Building), and a bistro in Forfar. The tip of a lexical iceberg, I suspect.

cliché

The origin of this word in the world of printing has long been forgotten, along with the technology that gave rise to it. It arrived in English in the early nineteenth century from French *clicher*, a verb meaning to 'make an impression on a surface of molten metal'. This would produce a cast or plate that would then be used for printing images. The plate was called the *cliché*. There's no earlier history to the word, which seems to suggests that it began as an imitation of the shushing sound made in the process.

It took a while for the modern meaning of an 'overused expression' to emerge. The earliest citation in the *Oxford English Dictionary* is 1881. Thereafter it attracted such derogatory adjectives as 'trite', 'facile', 'worn-out' and 'stale'. And it wasn't long before an associated sense appeared: any person, object or idea thought to be unoriginal was called a *cliché*, or attracted the adjective *clichéd*. The spelling was always contentious: to accent or not to accent? Many didn't like the word's French appearance, but to omit the accent resulted in a form that looked as if it should be pronounced 'kleesh'. There were humorous suggestions to get round the problem, such as *clitch*, but none caught on.

Clichés have always had a bad press. But it's not a straightforward issue. People have different views about whether a particular expression is a cliché or not. There are occasions when a cliché is actually useful, such as to fill an embarrassing silence. And it's not easy to avoid them, because of their colloquial smoothness. As a writer in *Readers' Digest* wryly remarked in a 1978 issue: 'I used to use clichés all the time, but now I avoid 'em like the plague.'

close the book (on) *see* **shut** *or* **close the book(s)**
closed book *see* **open and closed book**

code

This was one of thousands of words that came into English from French in the Middle Ages. The French got it from Latin *codex*, which began life as a tree trunk, then a wooden writing tablet, and then was used for books containing lists of accounts, laws, regulations and the like. The English use followed a similar development in its early years, but by the sixteenth century it had moved in a new direction. It began to refer to a set (often unwritten) of social conventions and expectations. People would talk about a 'code of manners', a 'code of honour', a 'code of fashions'. That's come down to us today, when companies talk about 'industrial codes', professions talk about 'codes of practice', and people ask, before an event, 'Is there a dress code?'

Since the eighteenth century there's been a veritable explosion of meanings. One strand has produced the various systems of signs and signals, including entities that replace letters or words, such as flag codes on ships and Morse code. The communicative function also varied: to facilitate communication (as with semaphore) or to keep it secret (as with ciphers). Another strand was in the sporting world, where different versions of a sport would be referred to as codes, as in the distinction between the rules of rugby union and rugby league. A third cluster led to specialized senses in botany, genetics, computing and other technical domains. Derivatives such as *encode* and *decode* arrived. Linguistics was influenced too: some linguists would talk about individual varieties or dialects of a language as 'codes', or even whole languages, as in the term 'code switching', when a bilingual speaker mixes two (or more) languages in a single sentence.

In everyday life, the commonest encounters with codes are in the domains of communications (dialling codes, country codes, zipcodes, post-codes…), security (access codes, entry codes, pass-codes…) and product management (barcodes, QR (quick-response) codes, discount codes…). And, of course, tax codes.

commonplace

The word goes back to Latin, *locus communis*, and earlier to Greek. It seems that writers have always felt the need to jot down short extracts from their reading, or ideas and reflections prompted by their life and times. The genre includes notebooks, journals, memo pads and diaries. They are, in effect, personal databases, plotting a private intellectual journey.

The word first appears in English in the sixteenth century, used for a passage in a text thought to be of special note – something that could fuel a discussion or a speech. At the same time, people began to make collections of these passages, copying them out and putting them into a notebook (or *table*) for future reference. They would include personal thoughts or ideas, as famously illustrated by Hamlet, in the first act of Shakespeare's play, who reflects that someone (his uncle) can 'smile and smile and be a villain', and decides to write this down in his 'tables'. *Commonplace books*, as they came to be called, became especially popular after the arrival of printing, which offered so many more reading sources than before.

It was a natural semantic development to see the word becoming used to mean an everyday saying or a statement of the obvious: 'it's a commonplace to say...' By the seventeenth century it had developed an adjectival use for anything felt to be ordinary or usual: 'a commonplace event'. And then, a century later, we see the emergence of a depreciative sense: anything uninteresting or unoriginal would be disparaged as 'commonplace'.

Today the function of a commonplace book is simulated online by blogs, tweets and all sorts of personal databases. When organized, such

as through the use of hashtags, we see a new
phenomenon: a shared commonplace site, where a
source remark elicits reactions from others. Several
apps now offer a personal note-taking service –
which of course can be made available so that
anyone can see them. The medium has its critics,
as it's not always easy to find your way around a vast
collection of online pages. I know some digerati
who value the small size of the traditional paper
commonplace book, with its flexibility, succinctness
and selectivity.

cook the books

Cook, as a noun, is one of the oldest words in
English, borrowed from Latin *cocus* in Anglo-Saxon
times, though – surprisingly – not recorded as a verb
until the fourteenth century. It soon developed a
number of figurative senses clustering around the
notion of preparing or 'eating' something other
than food. One might 'cook' words, for instance,
such as the commandments of the Bible, meaning to
savour them. By the seventeenth century we see *cook*
being used – along with *cook up* – in a negative way,
suggesting an intention to deceive or falsify, and to

surreptitiously alter facts in a way that wouldn't be noticed. Fake news, we'd say today.

It took a while before *cooking the books* arrived, in the sense of fraudulently altering financial records in account books. Its first recorded use is 1850. But its popularity has since soared, with the neat rhyme making the expression appeal in all sorts of circumstances. Cook The Books has named an Irish racehorse, for instance, and a Liverpool pop group of the 1980s – also known as Cook Da Books. Then, as so often happens with idioms, the literal sense of one of the words offers enticing opportunities for language play. So we find a 2007 British television series called *Cooking the Books*, whose aim was 'to bring recipes to life'. And online today there is Cook the Books, 'a community for cookbook enthusiasts'.

copy

In Latin, *copia* meant 'abundance', 'plenty', and this is how the word came into English in the fourteenth century. People would talk about 'great copy': 'Spain has great copy and plenty of castles', wrote the translator John Trevisa. The related word *copious* kept that meaning. Note that it was *great copy*, not *a great copy* – in linguistic terms, a mass noun (also called an uncountable noun). But the countable use developed at more or less the same time; so we find *a copy*, referring to an individual instance. This was at first mainly found in relation to written language: a transcript of some original text. But by the sixteenth century we find paintings and other works of art being copied too.

That century also shows a range of figurative uses clustering around the idea of an imitation. When Leonato says, in the last act of Shakespeare's *Much Ado About Nothing*, 'My brother hath a daughter, / Almost the copy of my child that's dead', he means a close likeness – the 'spitting image', we'd say today. There's no suggestion of exact identity.

The twentieth century saw another application in radio communication, especially in military settings. You send me a message. I respond with 'copy that'. All I mean is that I've heard and understood your message. It's just an acknowledgement, not an agreement or a commitment to act, and it's developed a new life in email exchanges.

It was a short step from here to leave the original source behind, as in the commonest sense today. When someone talks about 'a copy of a newspaper', for example, all they mean is that they have an individual instance of it. It wouldn't make much sense to try to identify a first version from which all the others have been reproduced.

An unusual reversal of meaning took place in the early modern period: *copy* came to mean 'that which is copied' – in other words, the *original* text from which copies would be made. The uncountable usage returned: authors supplied publishers 'with copy', and publishers supplied printers 'with copy'. Advertising agencies have *copywriters*. Journalists send 'copy' to their editors. The entries I'm writing will be 'the copy' from which will be produced 'the copy' you are reading now. They will have been checked by a 'copy-editor'. No wonder second-language learners of English get confused!

copybook *see* **blot one's copybook**
cover *see* **judging a book by its cover**

dab hand

Dab is a word that has sparked a great deal of debate. It arrived in English in the fourteenth century, meaning to 'strike' someone, especially with a light blow. If an implement was used, this would be soft, like a brush. The word had no previous history in English, and there seems to be no parallel in related languages. So it may well have been an action-associated sound formation, the vocal organs counterpointing the movement of the body.

Whatever the origin, a later semantic development is clear. During the eighteenth century we see it used in printing for the process of patting ('dabbing') a surface (such as a block of type) with ink or a colour so that it spreads evenly. It was quite a skilful job, so I rather like the view that the instrument used, or the person using it, or both, would be referred to as a 'dab hand'. Certainly by the early nineteenth century the expression was being used to describe anyone specially skilled at a task or in handling an implement.

The distinction between the tool and the person is still a feature of the idiom. If you're a dab hand *at* something, the emphasis is on the nature of the task. If you're a dab hand *with* something, the focus is on the device you're using to carry it out.

deadline

Has any word from the book world generated more drama titles than this one? Wikipedia lists over forty instances, dating from the 1920s, where it's been used as the title for a film or play. Unsurprisingly, a good number of them are crime or horror films, where the wordplay on time and death evidently proved irresistible to the writers.

The mortality theme was there from the very beginning, when the word was first used, in the 1860s. There was some usage where *dead* meant simply 'absence of motion' (as in 'come to a dead stop'): a static fishing line was called a deadline, for instance. But there was also a military usage: a boundary line around a prison which prisoners were not allowed to cross. If they did, they were liable to be shot. It was first used in the American Civil War, at the Confederate prisoner-of-war camp Andersonville.

It was this sense of a 'dangerous limit' that began to spread, at first in the USA. There were social deadlines that shouldn't be crossed. And by the 1920s it was being used in the publishing industry. A deadline was a time – a date or a time of day – by which a piece of writing had to be ready if it was to be included in a particular issue of a publication or to meet the demands of a publishing schedule. From there, the usage extended to any task or assignment – a time by which something needs to be done, such as preparing a meal or sending in a tax return.

When a commissioning editor gives a writer a deadline, there's an expectation that it will be respected. If only it were always so (says my Bodleian editor)! And there are famous cases of deadlines not being met, best summarized by Douglas Adams in *The Salmon of Doubt*: 'I love deadlines. I love the whooshing noise they make as they go by.' An informal usage was the consequence, after *drop dead!* began to be used in the 1930s as a strongly scornful expression. 'What's your drop-deadline?' an author might ask, having missed an initial deadline. It's a limit beyond which no further leeway will be granted. 'Can I have more time?' asks the hopeful writer, as that moment passes. 'Drop dead!'

dog-eared

It's not known who first saw the aptness of this metaphor, in the mid-eighteenth century, but once it was used it spread rapidly. There's something rather appealing about the way the ears of several breeds of dog flop down; but it's a mystery why the first user thought this was a good way of describing the way the top corner of a page is turned down to mark a place in a book. Soon after, the adjective became a verb, 'to dog-ear', which was also used in the sense of 'damage' or 'disfigure'. That proved not to be so popular, probably because the practice was often criticized, as once it's done the crease in the paper can't be eradicated.

By the end of the nineteenth century the adjective had developed a range of extended uses, being applied to anything thought to be worn out, hackneyed or shabby, and even to people who looked tired or exhausted. This use is still with us. Anyone who tells a well-known joke or describes something with a dull cliché might attract the label.

There's still quite a bit of life in the old metaphor. At least one company has hit on the idea of avoiding page damage by providing triangular bookmarks that slip over the top corner. And don't think that the notion is irrelevant in the online age. Some e-book readers have the option of adding a digital dog-ear. Tap the screen, and a small triangular mark pops up at the top corner. No damage at all now.

don't dip your pen in the company's ink *see* **pen**
every trick in the book *see* **books: imagined**

fine print

This is one of those expressions whose sense has become increasingly pejorative over the years. In the beginning – the mid-eighteenth century – it was a straightforward descriptive term, simply meaning a book or document that was printed in a small type size. An entire book might be printed in this way, and indeed the first recorded use of the expression names *The Book of Common Prayer* as an example. Poetry and magazines were other genres that tended to be in small print – or 'mouseprint', as it's sometimes called in ads these days.

A century later, the meaning of the expression had narrowed. It now referred to a section of text printed in a smaller type than the rest of a document. This contained extra information, supplementing what was in the body of the text. Footnotes (which had been around since the early 1700s) were an example. But the main use was to add a passage, usually at the end of a document, which contained material that was legally required, such as terms and conditions, and other content that would satisfy the need for 'full disclosure'. In books, the publishing data page is invariably in small print, and generally appears at the front, after the title page – though countries vary in their practice.

The negative sense began to emerge when it became apparent that the fine print was being used to hide important information. It was assumed – correctly, as it turned out – that most people wouldn't bother to read anything in fine print, and there have been many cases where people have entered into an agreement or purchased a product where they've been misled. Warnings appeared. 'Don't forget to read the fine print.' 'Check there's nothing hidden in the fine print.'

The final stage, to date, was when the expression transferred to non-text situations, meaning 'pay attention to the details'. So we hear such comments as 'Did you notice the fine print?', referring to a significant or contentious phrasing in a politician's speech. And, in an ironic twist, people might talk about 'reading the small print' even when it is large. I saw a theatre programme once in which there was a warning about the play's content – in big letters – and I heard someone ask their companion if they'd read the small print.

foolscap

The word looks like 'fool's cap' – and that's indeed what it was. In the fifteenth century, when this size of paper was introduced, the watermark chosen by European printers was the head of a jester wearing a multi-pointed fool's cap with bells. Britain changed it to an image of Britannia at the end of the eighteenth century, but the old name stayed.

The actual size varied among countries and according to purpose. Foolscap used for printing was roughly 8 × 13 inches (20 × 33 cm) – a little larger than the size used for handwriting. It was a popular choice for writing documents and official records, as the large size meant that not so many sheets were needed. Paper was expensive. Authors liked it too, for the same reason. And it was a highly popular size for letter writers during the eighteenth and nineteenth centuries, because it offered the writer a generous space before the sheet was folded and sealed. It's important to appreciate the size of the paper when there are allusions to it by authors from the time. Walter Scott, for example, began to keep a diary, and on 6 January 1826 he writes:

> I am annoyed beyond measure with the idle intrusion of voluntary correspondents; each man

who has a pen, ink, and sheet of foolscap to spare flies a letter at me.

They will have been long letters if they were using foolscap. No wonder he was cross.

Eventually, when the A4 size of paper became the industry standard in 1975, the use of foolscap markedly diminished. However, present-day suspension folders in filing cabinets are usually wide enough to comfortably take foolscap sheets, and foolscap box files, document wallets, ring binders and other stationery are still produced, so the word is in no danger of disappearing from everyday use.

four-letter word

I think I'm on safe ground if I assert that anyone reading this book doesn't need telling what the English words are, or why they're used or avoided. But listing them all isn't as straightforward as might appear. Does it include longer words, such as *bloody*? Does it include words from past times, such as *tush* and *pish*? The range of the expression has changed quite a lot since it was first used, towards the end of the nineteenth century. What words were excluded then from polite use? As well as those for sexual and excretory organs and functions, they included *damn*, *hell* and – surprisingly to modern ears – *liar*. Gilbert and Sullivan satirized the first of these in *HMS Pinafore*, as the Captain addresses his crew:

CAPTAIN	Bad language or abuse,
	I never, never use,
	Whatever the emergency;
	Though 'Bother it' I may
	Occasionally say,
	I never use a big, big D—.
ALL	What never?
CAPTAIN	No, never
ALL	What never?
CAPTAIN	Well, hardly ever!

The earliest use of the expression so far recorded is much older. It's an adjective, 'four-lettered', and it turns up in the seventeenth century in a book called *The Glory of Women*, a translation of a Latin text by Henricus Cornelius Agrippa, asserting the pre-eminence of women over men – a remarkable exception to the male-dominated climate of the time. He writes: 'the name of woman hath more affinity with that unspeakable four-letter'd name of the divine omnipotency, then [than] the name of man.' He's referring to the Hebrew name for God, known as the tetragrammaton, and conventionally spelled YHWH (and often written Yahweh).

Today, the usage goes well beyond the obscene. Book titles especially attract it, such as *Love is a Four-Letter Word*. Replace *Love* by *Life, Hero, Wait, Fear, Work*... and many more. And not forgetting the negations, such as *Suicide is not a Four-Letter Word*. Nor, to my mind, the crowning glory in this genre: *No is a Four-Letter Word*.

front-page news *see* **jump off the page**

gloss

The world of publishing has given us two senses, which occasionally overlap: one visual, one linguistic. The visual one is slightly older. In the sixteenth century we see it in the sense of a 'superficial lustre', along with the adjective, used in contexts that suggest something smooth, shiny or highly polished. It was probably borrowed from one of the Germanic family of languages; words like *glass* and *glow* are related. It was an obvious candidate for figurative development, and in the following century we see it describing anything that seemed attractive, with the implication that the lustrous appearance was hiding a reality. It was often used as a verb with *over*: to 'gloss over' something, physically or in words, would suggest a deception.

The visual sense went in a new direction in the twentieth century. In the 1930s, photographic paper that was smooth and shiny came to be described as 'glossy', and so were the travel brochures and magazines printed on such paper. A decade later and the mags were being called 'glossies', and in the 1960s so were films about fashionable life – Hollywood glossies. An idiom arose: to 'take the gloss off' something was to reduce its value.

While all this was going on, a linguistic sense of *gloss* was also evolving, in the sixteenth century, from an earlier word *gloze*, and strongly influenced by Latin *glossa*, meaning a word that requires explanation. Glosses of difficult or foreign words would be inserted into the margin or between the lines of a text. Some of the earliest writings in English are the Anglo-Saxon glossaries (Latin into English) from around the seventh century. This was another candidate for figurative development, and during the seventeenth century we see the verb being used in various negative meanings, such as 'make unfavourable remarks about someone' or 'comment superficially'. *Over* appears again: if I 'gloss over' something, I'm not going into it in depth, and perhaps I'm hiding something.

So when you see the idiom 'gloss over', you have two meanings competing for your attention. Which is it – visual or vocal? Often it's impossible to say.

good books *see* **books: imagined**
gospel truth *see* **take as gospel**

graffiti

The word is surprisingly recent. The first recorded instance found to date is in 1954, referring to words or drawings on walls or other surfaces made without permission in a public place. They might be written, brush-painted, paint-sprayed or scratched – and it's this last technique that links the English word to its history, for it comes from Italian *graffito* meaning 'a little scratch'.

The Italian word has an illustrious past, reflecting a behaviour that can be traced back to ancient times, such as the graffiti found on walls in the ruins of Pompeii. It also describes a traditional method of decoration in which the artist scratches through a surface layer (such as plaster) to reveal a different colour. Both senses arrived in English in the mid-nineteenth century, and we see such terms as 'graffito pottery', and in more recent times graffito wallpaper, fabrics and prints – 'art graffiti' (or 'graffiti art'). Books of graffiti texts have also proved popular, notably those collected by Nigel Rees.

The word has come to be used as both a singular and a plural: we hear not only *graffiti*, meaning a multiplicity of markings, but *a graffiti*, meaning a single instance – something that attracts pedantic ire, with critics insisting that it should be *a graffito*. The social issue of course is much more controversial than the linguistic point. 'Is it art, protest or vandalism?' was a *Times* headline a few years ago. 'Graffiti is always vandalism' headed a *New York Times* piece. But when a piece by Banksy sells for over a million pounds, the issue is evidently more complicated.

gutter press *see* **hot off the press**
have your nose in a book *see* **bookworm**

headline

The concept of a text *head line*, written as two words, has some interesting origins. In the seventeenth century it was being used in relation to handwriting. Letters such as *a, c, e* ... would be written between an imaginary 'head line' and a base line. The loops for *b, d, g* ... would extend above or below these lines. Some teachers would actually draw the lines on the page, to help learners. The practice was especially popular in the nineteenth century, and I imagine some teachers still follow it.

Then, in the eighteenth century, printers used the term to describe the area at the top of a page where there would be a running title and a page number. The first line of text on the page was also often called the *head line* – again, as two words. And when the term extended to its modern meaning, towards the end of that century, it was again written as two words – sometimes spaced, sometimes hyphenated – before settling down in the form *headline*.

The typographical prominence given to a headline, drawing attention to the content of the writing that followed, soon motivated a dynamic spoken idiom, which began in America around 1900: to 'make the headlines', and then more dramatically, 'hit the headlines'. It would be used for any piece of news thought to be especially noteworthy – whether it actually appeared in print or not. Or it might just be a startling event: somebody drops a dish on the floor, and an observer says 'That'll hit the headlines!'

In the 1920s we find the term transferring to the spoken medium, with the arrival of radio broadcasting: people would hear an announcer 'speaking the headlines' of a news bulletin. 'I'm just listening to the headlines', they might say. And then, with the introduction of television, we find another visual sense: 'I'm watching the headlines', where the viewer may not see anything in print at all, only a newsreader.

hot off the press

This is one of the most misunderstood idioms from the book world. Innumerable sources say that it comes from the days when newsprint was produced by molten lead poured into a mould to make a printing block. But this technology didn't develop until the late nineteenth century, and the first recorded use of this expression (as 'hot from the press') is long before that, in 1804. *Hot* applied to news or information is much older, used in the sixteenth century to mean something fresh, novel or exciting – news that arrives very soon after an event. The *Oxford English Dictionary* has found a first recorded use of 'hot newes' in 1569. Doubtless hot-metal printing gave the expression a fresh force, and its use certainly became more frequent in the late nineteenth century; but that's not where it originated. This is an excellent example of the way historical citations in lexicography can correct a linguistic myth.

'Hot off the press' still has its meaning of 'newly published', but it's also now widely used to mean simply 'new' or 'newly received', without any reference to newsprint. A further implication is that the news is not only new but sensational, and it's this connotation that has given it an appeal in other contexts. I've found it naming a thermal protection hair spray, a natural cleansing shampoo, a slot game, a racehorse, and – cleverly – a dry-cleaning service in Glasgow.

The potential of the press to provide sensational news is also there in a related idiom: the 'gutter press'. *Gutter* came into English from French in the thirteenth century, meaning a watercourse, and was soon used in connection with buildings, referring to a channel for carrying off rainwater and filth. It was the latter sewerage-related sense that led to it being used in the twentieth century for newspapers that published sensational or scandalous stories about the private lives of celebrities. It's generally used in a negative way. No hair shampoo naming here.

icon

People born into the digital age live in a world of icons – the small clickable images on a screen that have a specific function, such as (on websites) a link to an application or another page or (in emails) the array at the top of a message that allows you to reply, forward, delete, get mail, mark as spam, and so on. Some icons can't be selected, but simply represent an entity, such as a company. Whatever their function, one thing is clear: there are an awful lot of them. One website offers half a million icon designs.

It's a long way from here to the word's original meaning. In the context of computing it's been around only since the 1980s. The original sense arrived in English in the sixteenth century, from Latin, and earlier Greek, where it meant an image or likeness of something. The first English uses were especially for illustrations of animals, birds and plants, as well as for personal portraits and written descriptions – what today we would call *similes*. A little later we find memorial statues and busts described as 'icons'. Then, in the eighteenth century, the religious usage emerged: a colourful representation of a holy person which itself would be regarded as sacred and an object of adoration.

We have to wait until the 1950s before we encounter the other main modern use of the word, outside the world of computing, along with the even more recent (in the 1970s) adjective, *iconic*. We're now in the company of Elvis Presley, Marilyn Monroe, Princess Diana, the Beatles, Harley-Davidson, Big Ben, the Eiffel Tower, and innumerable other widely known people or things thought to represent a culture, place, genre, period of time or social movement. In situations such as advertising, consumer magazines, pop music and television shows, a celebrity or product can be widely praised as 'iconic' – meaning only that, in the view of the originator, it's the best of its kind (but of course with the unspoken hope that it will become iconic in the earlier sense). If you would like to emulate them, there are now dozens of online sites with such titles as 'How to Become an Icon'. Good luck!

impression

The word had quite a long history before it came to be used in printing: the notion of one thing pressing on the surface of another dates from the fifteenth century. It came in from French, and earlier Latin, in the sense of pressing or stamping; and soon after William Caxton introduced the new technology into Britain it was being used to refer to the general process of printing. From there it narrowed to mean a particular instance of printing: an individual sheet or copy. And it was then applied to all the copies printed on a particular occasion, such as a first edition or a reprint. People would talk about a 'first impression', a 'second impression' and so on.

At the same time as the word was developing its physical senses, it was also being used for mental activity. The pressing was now on our mind – the effect of perceiving something that makes us think or feel in a certain way. And what a range of impressions came from this perspective! Here are just some of the impressions we give, make, form, create, leave… They can relate to time (first, immediate, early, initial, fleeting, lasting…), range (general, overall, widespread, main, overwhelming, overriding…), strength (deep, indelible, powerful, strong, superficial, vivid, firm, clear, convincing...), veracity (good, accurate, positive, subjective, distinct... false, wrong, misleading, mistaken, erroneous, distorted, negative...), and many more.

The word continues to make new ripples, especially in the online world. In the field of advertising, an 'impression' is a metric used to calculate the number of times an ad, post or page has been viewed. Advertisers want to know how often possible customers have chosen to look at their ad. A new expression has evolved to capture the payment made by the advertiser when this happens; CPI – 'cost per impression'. The numbers can be enormous, so that expressions such as 'million impressions' are routine now, in this world.

ink

It's such a small word that its origin in the imposing Latin form *encaustum*, and its earlier Greek equivalent, may cause some surprise. It described the special purple-red liquid used ceremonially by Roman and Greek emperors for their signatures, obtained from the coverings of certain shellfish, heated to form a fluid (hence the name, which was literally 'in burning' in Greek). It arrived in French in a shortened form – *encre* today – and came into English as one of the imports from France in the thirteenth century.

The fluid could be dyed with many colours, but its default form was black, as suggested by the simile that emerged by the sixteenth century: 'as black as ink', usually referring literally to the perceived colour of some object, such as the weather or the water in a lake. But the word also had a figurative application: crimes and sins could be described as 'inky', and it was also applied to wicked or mean-spirited people, who would have souls 'spotted with ink'.

Ink as a writing fluid is unusual today. Inkpots, inkstands and other equipment are largely things of the past. But the word lives on in the electronic world, with inkjet printers. And since the early years of the twentieth century we've used it when talking metaphorically about the amount of newspaper or other publicity coverage for a topic or event. The ink is now being 'spilled' or 'spent'. 'A lot of ink has been spent on...' frequently introduces an article – in which more ink is about to be spent.

in someone's book *see* **books: imagined**

jot

Jot arrived in English thanks to translations of the Bible – first by a group associated with John Wycliffe in the late fifteenth century, and then by William Tyndale in the early sixteenth. The relevant passage is in the Gospel of St Matthew (chapter 5, verse 18): in Tyndale's original spelling, 'For truely I saye vnto you till heven and erth perisshe one iott or one tytle of the lawe shall not scape tyll all be fulfilled.' The spelling *iott* points to the origin of the word. It comes from the name of the smallest letter in the Greek alphabet, *iota* (pronounced iy-*oh*-ta) – smallest, because it takes only one stroke to write it. (There was no dot over the *i* in Greek.) The expression 'not one jot', and then 'not a jot', reflected that meaning: 'the least or tiniest amount of something'. There's always a 'not' or some other negative word nearby.

Judging by the many citations from the time, it proved to be a very useful word. Shakespeare liked it a lot: he uses it twenty-three times, and puts it into the mouths of some of his most prominent characters, such as Hamlet, Othello, Portia and King Lear. Portia, for example, cleverly points out (in the climactic Act 4 of *The Merchant of Venice*) that Shylock's intention to take a pound of flesh from Antonio 'doth give thee here no jot of blood'.

But Shakespeare doesn't use the other word with which *jot* is most often associated, as in the Matthew quotation: *tittle*. It was another classical word, this time from Latin, *titulus* – *title* has the same origin. It meant a dot or other small mark used in writing or printing – such as a punctuation mark or a diacritic. The whole expression 'no jot or tittle' was thus really emphatically negative: if *jot* was 'not a bit', *jot and tittle* was 'not the slightest bit'.

journal

The story of this word is one of slow and steady broadening of meaning. It arrived in English from French in the sixteenth century, with the specific sense of 'every day'. The Duke in Act 4 of Shakespeare's *Measure for Measure* talks about the sun making a 'journal greeting' – a daily appearance. As a noun, it had a growing range of 'book' applications. In religious settings it was a type of service book. In the context of travel it was a record of someone's journey – what today we'd call an itinerary. In the business world it was a daily record of commercial transactions. In shipping it was a logbook. And it was widely used in both private and official circles as a daybook – a sort of diary, but with much more detail.

It's not until the eighteenth century that we see the word approaching its present-day meaning. It included any daily publication, such as a newspaper, periodical or gazette. Today it's chiefly used for periodicals, especially in academia, but any kind of magazine may still be called a journal, and even the occasional newspaper. There's a daily paper called *The Journal* in north-east England, and in the north of Scotland people can read *The Press and Journal*, another daily regional paper.

The digital domain has brought a fresh cluster of applications. A 'bullet journal' is a method of organizing one's reminders, schedules and suchlike. There are many 'journalling' apps available now – the eighteenth-century word 'journalizing' seems to have died out – along with guides about how you go about creating an online journal. But the broadest application I've seen is a website which calls itself The Journal Shop. It sells anything related to the world of written composition – stationery, pens, notebooks, planners, and all sorts of writing equipment. The word has travelled a long way from its comfortable 'daily' origins.

judging a book by its cover

The concept is old. In *Macbeth*, Shakespeare has King Duncan reflect on the traitorous Thane of Cawdor, whom he had trusted: 'There's no art to find the mind's construction in the face.' Appearances can be deceiving, as the proverb says. The book-related idiom isn't recorded until the mid-nineteenth century, though it was anticipated in 1704 by Irish poet Edmund Arwaker, who wrote in a preface to his translation of *Aesop's Fables*: 'a Man is not to be judg'd of by his Out-side, any more than a Book by its Title-Page'. He was making the point that there's more to those fables than might appear at first sight.

It's the negative sense that became proverbial: *never* (or *don't, you can't*) *judge a book by its cover* – or, in some versions, *its binding*. The warning is not to make assumptions about something or someone (as another idiom suggests: 'at face value'). Any external feature can evoke it: a person's hair or dress, the way food looks on a plate, an off-putting shop frontage...

Inevitably, some writers have gone in the opposite direction. Steven Jenkins is one, in his *Cheese Primer* (1996), commenting on artisanal cheeses which 'are usually much scruffier on the outside than factory-made ones', and concluding: 'Choosing a cheese is one of the few times you should judge a book by its cover.' Publishers, too, are suspicious of the negative tradition, knowing the value of a striking cover design. And the impact of a book cover is felt to be especially important on social media sites that offer book publicity. As a *Guardian* article put it in 2021: 'In the Instagram age, you actually can judge a book by its cover.'

jump off the page

During the nineteenth century, as newspapers became more frequent, their style more eye-catching, and their headlines more dramatic, idioms such as this one attempted to capture the excitement of news stories, where the words or images are so vivid that they immediately catch your attention. The content of an article might jump off the page too, in the sense that it would pique your interest or capture your imagination. You might be reading a table of athletics results, for instance, when suddenly one strikes you as especially impressive, or reminds you of something.

Page also appears in another idiom that emerged during that century, expressing a notion of excitement: 'front-page news'. It was the front page that was the critical thing, as that was where the most noteworthy stories (in the view of the editor) were to be found. So we also find 'front-page headlines', 'front-page story', and other variants. The idiomatic function was clear when people started to use these expressions without having any actual front page in mind. All they meant was that some event or other was worthy of appearing on a front page. The actual event might of course be quite trivial, and the speaker might be being ironic. 'It's snowing' might elicit the remark. And I recall 'Hey, front-page news!' from a parent. Her child had just lost a first tooth.

One more, from the same century. How to report a memorable event in a person's life or in the story of a country? 'It was a bright page when...' perhaps; or 'a dark page...' The adjectives vary, but the implication is clear. The event would fill a page if it were written in a history book.

As a footnote, I think it's worth recording that 'jump off the page' has, since the 1920s, acquired a literal meaning, thanks to pop-up books. And, with 3D printing, visual reality goggles and digital holograms, who knows what the future will bring.

leaf

This little word has evidently had great popular appeal, for it has generated four idiomatic expressions based on its sense of a sheet of paper in a book or other document. It's been in English from the very beginning, in Anglo-Saxon times – one of those basic words that appears in all Germanic languages, and with an earlier history that takes it back to the first Indo-European tongues. It's probably related to Latin *liber*, meaning both 'book' and 'the inner bark of a tree', which was used as a writing material in Greek and Roman times.

The earliest recorded idiom in English is *turn over a leaf* in the mid-sixteenth century, with *new* added soon after, which is how we use it today, meaning to adopt a different – and hopefully better – course of action. 'Glad to see David's turned over a new leaf.' In the seventeenth century appears *turn down a leaf*, both in its literal sense of folding the top corner of a page to mark a place in a book, and then figuratively to mean making a mental note of something in order to come back to it. In the eighteenth century we find *take a leaf out of someone's book*, meaning to follow the example of another person. There's also *borrow a leaf...*, heard especially in American English. It's used in the plural as well:

We're all going to turn over new leaves next year. And then, in the nineteenth, *leaf through* emerged for the action of going through the pages in a book, or the papers in a pile, in a casual way, largely replacing an earlier *leaf over*.

It's interesting to see how the *turn over* idiom has returned to its literal roots in playful headlines for articles, especially about cookery or gardening. This was the heading for a piece about the way earthworms make a useful mulch for fruit trees out of fallen leaves: 'Worms turn over new leaves for orchardists'. An article about a new recipe for salad was headed 'Turn over new leaves'. And one of the best puns I've seen was on a government poster from the Second World War, now on display in the Imperial War Museum in London: 'TURN OVER A NEW LEAF: Eat Vegetables daily to enjoy good health.'

leaflet

The term began in botany, in the eighteenth century, where it described a leaf-like part of a compound leaf – a 'little leaf'. The notion evidently appealed to writers, as a century later we see it adopted – in 1852 in volume 96 of a literary periodical, *The New Monthly Magazine and Humorist* – to describe short biographical articles. The pieces were called *Literary Leaflets*, and they became a regular feature of the magazine for fifteen years.

Meanwhile, the notion of shortness took the term in a different direction, as the publishing world responded to the demand for new formats. We see the first use of *booklet* in 1859, and a year later the even shorter *leaflet* – a single sheet of printed paper, folded or unfolded, used especially as part of an advertising or political campaign, and free of charge. By the end of the century it had become a verb: *to leaflet*, meaning to publish something in this form; and the people who wrote them or distributed them were *leafleteers*.

The effectiveness of leaflets continued into the twentieth century. The 1930s brought *leaflet raid* – from aeroplanes dropping them into enemy territory. The 1940s added *leaflet drop*, for a planned distribution in an area. *Leafletting* as a noun appeared in 1945. And the later decades showed an extraordinary growth, with medical, educational, charitable and other public domains displaying a wide variety of leaflets, often in several languages. The designs became more creative, with colour, shiny finish, bullet points, prominent headlines and logos, striking images, and other effects that urged readers to act and respond.

And now we have *digital leaflets*. Do you want to – as one website puts it – 'showcase your brand, products and services in an easy-to-read format online'? Several companies offer design facilities and templates that enable organizations to tell the world about themselves in a succinct manner – much shorter than a company website or a digital brochure. And virtually all of the spam that comes into my inbox has the character of a leaflet. The electronic world hasn't replaced the physical one, by any means – two came through my front door this week, advertising local businesses – but it has certainly given the term fresh energy.

lexicon

My earliest encounter with this word was as a child, when I learned to play a card game called Lexicon – a word-building game in the same genre as Scrabble, with letters having different values, and a highly desirable Master Card which could stand for any letter. The word has been in English since the sixteenth century, a borrowing from Latin, and earlier Greek, where it comes from *lexis* 'word'. It was used to describe a dictionary, or word book, at first with reference to ancient languages, and then for any language.

It next developed the sense of a listing of the words used in a particular domain, such as a region, profession or genre, or the vocabulary of a single person or social group. Or a topic: we see such expressions as 'the lexicon of love'. In modern times it has a technical sense in linguistics: all the meaningful units in a language. The entire vocabulary of a language is described as its 'lexicon'.

These are understandable word-based developments. What is mysterious is the way *lexicon* has acquired a popular appeal, naming entities that – on the surface at least – have nothing at all to do with words There are 164 businesses listed in the UK's Companies House (as of the beginning of 2024) with Lexicon as their name, or a part of their name. I take three at random: a pharmaceuticals company, a security and surveillance company, and a major shopping complex in Bracknell, Berkshire. There are more online, such as a library management site for professional DJs. And not forgetting the blends that have been created from it, resulting in such company names as Lexiconsulting, Lexiconomist and Lexiconstruction. As there are hundreds of words in English beginning with *con-*, I suspect that these are just a fraction of the names that have been coined over the years.

libel

The word came from French in the fourteenth century, with an earlier origin in Latin, *libellus*, from *liber* with a diminutive ending: 'little book'. And that's what it meant in its earliest English uses: a short piece of writing on some subject, or a formal document containing some sort of declaration. During the Middle Ages it began to be used in legal contexts, such as a plaintiff's written statement of the charges that would initiate a lawsuit.

We don't see the modern use until the 1600s: any published writing that damages someone's reputation – one of the two kinds of defamation (the other being slander, for spoken offences). It also had a broader meaning, referring to any piece of writing thought to be treasonable or immoral.

It seems unlikely that such a serious legal term would develop any unexpected usage, but there was one. In the early sixteenth century a long poem appeared which was widely circulated, titled *Vox Populi Vox Dei* ('the voice of the people [is] the voice

of God'). It was an anonymous complaint against
taxation written in the style of poet John Skelton
(the tutor of Prince Henry, later Henry VIII). It's
addressed 'To the Kinges moste Exellent Maiestie'
(presumably Henry VII), and in its opening lines it
states its aim:

> The trothe to tell you playne
> Of all those that do holde
> The substance and the golde,
> And the treasure of this realme…

And among these people, in Book 12 we find the
first collective noun for the legal profession: 'a hole
libell of lawyers'.

little black book

Books are often identified by their coloured covers,
especially when they provide a guide to something.
The UK government has a Blue Book of fishing
regulations, a Green Book on vaccines, an Orange
Book on risk management, and so on. Such publications don't usually develop any idiomatic use
outside of their original domains, but as soon as we
encounter a colour with 'little' preceding, everything

changes. *The Quotations from Chairman Mao Tse-tung* (1964) became known colloquially as the 'Little Red Book'. But nothing matches the outreach of the 'little black book'.

Although any official book bound in black would attract this label, modern popular usage can be traced back to the sixteenth century, when it began to be used for a book listing the names of people liable to be censured or punished. By the eighteenth century it was being personalized in a related idiom: 'to be in David's black book(s)' was to be out of favour with David.

Today 'little black book' has a mixed use. It can be simply an address book of important names or contact details. But it makes the headlines when the listing is of people with whom a celebrity has had an amorous relationship. And it named a 2004 satirical comedy film, along with the blurb: 'Have you ever been tempted to look inside his little black book?'

Not all instances are suggestive, though. Little Black Book can just name a helpful listing, as in *Country Life*'s 'online directory to help you find the people you can really trust to help you, your family and your home'. It's the title of Otegha Uwagba's 2016 bestseller, with the blurb 'a toolkit for working women'. It names several websites, such as the Little Black Book of London, providing 'bespoke accommodation services for the film and TV industry'. And when we look through the projects carrying this name, we see that the expression now satisfies the true test of an idiom, for the cover or home page of some of these 'black books' is no longer black.

logo

What has this to do with fishing baskets? *Logo* is probably a shortening of *logotype*, used in printing by hand in the nineteenth century: it was a single unit of type containing two or more letters, cast as a single piece – a great time-saving technique for very frequent words such as *the* and *of.* But also in that century we find *logogram* and *logograph*, used for any symbol that represented a word. Then, much earlier, in the sixteenth century we find *logogriph* for a kind of word puzzle where you form a word or phrase from the letters of another word or phrase. We'd call them anagrams today. Our modern *logo* shows the influence of all these alternatives.

It arrived in the 1960s, referring to any graphic symbol which was being used to identify an object, concept, organization, event, product, and so on. It included such everyday features as road signs, but it became especially associated with the world of advertising. However, the notion now extends well beyond the symbols associated with the big companies. There are many online sites that offer us the opportunity to create our own personal logo, if we feel we need to build a brand. They're popular. Some sites claim millions of clients.

And the fishing baskets? *Logogriph* came into English from French, and earlier from Greek *logos* 'word' + *griphos*, which meant a riddle – and also a fishing basket. Why? The reference is to its intricately woven character. Rhetoricians saw a parallel between it and any convoluted, incoherent or puzzling utterance.

lower case *see* **upper and lower case**

margin

This came into English from French in the fourteenth century. The French got it from Latin, where a *margo* was a border or edge of something, and that was its earliest meaning in English too. People would talk about the 'margin' or 'margins' of a field or a plate, then of a river bank or the seashore. The

Latin word was also used for the edge of a writing tablet or book, and English adapted this context to describe the border on either side of the text on a page. It was usually left empty, but writers and printers would sometimes use it to add a reference note of some kind, or perhaps a special feature, such as an illuminated letter.

The word came to be used in a wide range of settings, as expressions such as 'margin of error' and 'winning margin' suggest. But the book trade had its developments too. To say that something is 'in the margins' could literally refer to some information on a printed page, but more often it had an extended use, referring to something incidental. The adjective *marginal* went the same way, from a literal sense of 'on the edge' to its common present-day sense (but only since the 1950s) of 'minor importance'. We talk about something being of 'marginal interest' or having a 'marginal effect'.

Then in the nineteenth century we see the arrival of *marginalia*, another Latin borrowing, referring to any notes or comments written in a margin. Why do we do it? They're an emotional outlet for our feelings about what we're reading, and a note to ourselves about passages we think are important or personally meaningful. When these are by well-known authors they're seen as a valuable insight into the writers' way of thinking, and some are famous for their marginalia. Coleridge's, for instance, have been collected into five volumes. The phenomenon is widespread, and is probably universal among academics. George Steiner once defined an intellectual as 'a human being who has a pencil in his or her hand when reading a book'.

minutes

These days the word usually appears in the plural: 'the minutes of a meeting', meaning a brief official record or summary of what took place. But when it arrived in English in the fourteenth century from Latin, often via French, it was more often used in the singular. Latin *minutum* meant a small object, an unimportant thing, sometimes a coin or the sixtieth part of a unit; and all these notions appear in early English usage. When, during the following century, it started to be used with reference to writing, the notion of smallness was retained. In Latin, *scriptura minuta* was literally 'small writing', an expression describing when someone made a rough draft of something, or sent someone an informal note or memorandum.

The meaning gradually became more formal. By the end of the sixteenth century the term was being used in contexts requiring precision: a piece of writing giving instructions to someone would be called a 'minute'. By the eighteenth it was beginning to have the sense of a record of proceedings, and used both in the singular and in the plural. It's stayed that way ever since. The only linguistic development has been in relation to the classification of types of minute, though it's not clear just how widespread such terminology has become.

As well as a 'minute of record', we find a 'minute of dissent', noting someone's disagreement with a decision. A 'minute of consideration' recognizes that a point was discussed but not decided upon – the latter would be a 'minute of decision'. A 'minute of appointment' would specify relevant contractual details. A 'minute of report' would acknowledge the presentation of a report to the meeting. One always has to allow for incompleteness: if a meeting runs out of time, there will be a 'continued minute'. And a 'holding minute' is needed when a complex issue needs further discussion at a future meeting. These issues, if not the terminology, will certainly be recognized by anyone who has ever been given the task of 'taking the minutes'.

miscellany

This word first appeared in the late sixteenth century, with some writers borrowing it from Latin, and others from French. It had a meaning very like *anthology* – a collection of articles on a particular subject brought together to make a book. But the two words went in different directions. An anthology always aims to provide a judicious selection of texts that represent the best of a genre; a miscellany, by contrast, is a looser collection motivated chiefly by popular or commercial interests, and often including the quirky or unusual. Virtually anything might turn up in a book called *A Welsh Miscellany*, *A Shakespeare Miscellany* or *A Medical Miscellany*, as long as it has some plausible link with the subject. Some miscellanies have been bestsellers, such as those compiled by American author Ben Schott. And the Bodleian, of course, has published Claire Cock-Starkey's *The Book Lover's Miscellany* and *A Museum Miscellany*.

It wasn't long before the word left its bookish sense and began to be applied to a collection of any kind. Early uses include a miscellany of tunes, clothing and people. John Dryden describes Shakespeare's character Falstaff as 'a Miscellany of Humours or Images, drawn from so many several men'. And today we find it used for virtually anything that's countable: radio music shows, greetings cards, cooking ingredients, sculptures, celebrities... Artistic Miscellany is 'a website devoted to art and architecture, and museums and galleries in the United Kingdom and around the world'. A British folk dance group is called Young Miscellany. In 2014 the Bank of England mounted an exhibition: they called it *Curiosities from the vaults: a Bank miscellany*. And playful coinages have emerged. In 2023 the London law chambers Gray's Inn put on a Christmas show for its members. They called it The Christmiscellany.

not a jot *see* **jot**
nothing to write home about *see* **writing**
not worth the paper it's written on *see* **paper**
one for the book(s) *see* **books: imagined**

on/off the books

In the early years of the eighteenth century we see two related idioms emerging. 'On the books' came first, meaning to be on a list or register of an organization. It could be a company, society, club, team, agency... anything where membership involved a recognized or official status. 'I've at last managed to get on the books of an agent', a newly trained actor recently told me. Then, inevitably, by the mid-century there was the opposite, with a variety of verbs: one's name could be 'taken/struck/knocked... off the books'. A recent report of a record-breaking athlete failing a drugs test led to their name being 'struck off the books'.

A later use of the *on/off* prepositions went in a different direction, in relation to accounting and taxation. If you received payment for a job 'off the books', it would mean you'd been paid in cash, without any record of your role being made in the employer's account books. It's used adjectivally too: 'off-the-books labour', or a similar phrase, is likely to be found in any article on the 'underground' or 'shadow' economy of a country.

Employment is always an underlying notion in 'on the books' usages, and this is what distinguishes it from 'in the books', which usually means that an event or a piece of information has been officially recorded – and not necessarily in a physical book (perhaps an audio or video recording, or digitally – another example of **books: imagined**). Having said that, usage in the latter sense often varies. The American broadcasting company CBS in 2016 reported that December 2015 in Minnesota was 'the warmest on the books'. In February 2023 it said about New York: 'January went down in the books as the warmest on record.' Online searches bring up both usages in almost equal measure, these days. One of them may be the eventual victor, but it's too soon to predict which, and in any case British, American and other regional varieties of English will probably go in different directions, as has already happened with such cases as *on the weekend* (American) vs *at the weekend* (British), *in university* vs *at university*, and *Tuesday through Thursday* vs *Tuesday to Thursday*.

on paper *see* **paper**

on the same page

This is one of those idioms that has been condemned for overuse, especially in business contexts, where people have used it to express a sense of mutual understanding and working as a team. But in everyday speech, since its first recorded use in the mid-twentieth century, it's been quite a common way for two people to say they're in agreement about something: 'I think we're on the same page.' Or pages (which is the answer to the crossword puzzle clue in **bring to book** on page 27).

Even more ire has been heaped on an alternative group of expressions, of which 'we're singing from the same hymn sheet' is the most famous – a favourite of anyone (especially a politician) making a public policy statement or declaring a manifesto, and wanting to emphasize that there's a united front, especially when there have been previous signs of disagreement. This is older, with variants known since the mid-nineteenth century: 'using' instead of 'singing', 'song sheet' or 'tune' instead of 'hymn sheet'. But not everyone hates it: 'Singing from the same hymn sheet' heads a website page from a British business school, which then adds the gloss: 'an apt metaphor for team work'. And it was only a matter of time before an online company would emerge with the name Samepage, described as a 'business-oriented cloud service that provides social collaboration, file sharing and project management capabilities designed to help people work better together'.

As with many idioms, the literal meaning of the words can shine through when copywriters are looking for an eye-catching headline. Here's an example from the *Telegraph* during the pandemic, when some vicars cancelled festive services while others kept them: 'Churches not singing from the same hymn sheet over cancelling Christmas carols'. And if people aren't on the same page, or are uncertain about it? My favourite here is an Australian colloquialism: 'David is in the book but he doesn't know what page he's on'!

open and closed book

This is probably one of the most self-explanatory items in this collection, but with some unexpected applications and a puzzle. It seems to have begun with the seventeenth-century poet and playwright William Davenant, who used it in two of his poems, expressing the idea of a person who has a personality that's easy to understand, or who gives the impression of having nothing to hide. 'There's no mystery about me. I'm an open book', says George Bevan in P.G. Wodehouse's *A Damsel in Distress* (1919). 'My heart is an open book', sang crooners such as Carol Dobkins Jr, Dean Martin and Cliff Richard, following the song's release in 1959.

What's less obvious is to see the expression being used for things and situations. 'All nature is an open book…', wrote eighteenth-century hymn writer Isaac Watts, and he extends the metaphor: 'To spread her maker's praise abroad, / And every page on which we look / Shows something worthy of a God'. And we find it widely used in relation to anything that people find they are easily able to appreciate or understand, such as computers, art forms and social media.

Or the opposite, of course. 'TikTok is a closed book to me', a puzzled parent might say. The puzzle is why the idiom isn't recorded until the early twentieth century. Maybe earlier examples will be found one day. But its popularity has grown, and just the other day I heard it twice in ten seconds, in a conversation between a British shopkeeper and an American visitor. 'Baseball is a closed book to me', said the Brit. 'Not as closed as cricket is to me', riposted the American.

orphans *see* **widows**

out of sorts

The expression covers a multitude of conditions, both physical and mental, where we don't feel our normal self – everything from feeling slightly unwell to being in low spirits, or just feeling uncomfortable or irritated for some reason.

There's a widespread belief that it began in the world of printing. In typesetting, a *sort* is the technical name for a letter (or other character) in a particular fount of type. It's first recorded in 1668. In the days of manual typesetting, compositors took a sort from the two boxes containing upper-case and lower-case letters to make up the words in a text. As the boxes could hold only limited numbers of each letter, there would be occasions when they ran out, because the text they were setting used up all the sorts. Doubtless the expression *out of sorts* came into use then, but we don't actually see a recorded example until a century later. In February 1784 American writer (and printer) Benjamin Franklin wrote in a jocular vein to a friend in England about delays in the publication of government papers there: 'The founts too must be very scanty, or strangely out of sorts, since your compositors cannot find either upper or lower case letters sufficient to set the word ADMINISTRATION.'

The problem with the printing theory is that *out of sorts*, in its general sense, is well attested long before that. We see it first in 1621, when a writer expresses surprise about someone feeling 'out of tune or out of sorts'. And there are many other instances recorded before we get to Benjamin Franklin. Perhaps the technical sense of the idiom came from the general one – 'something abnormal in the box of sorts'. On the other hand, *sort* in its general sense of 'kind [of thing]' had been in English since the Middle Ages. So it's just as likely that the printing use was simply an extension of that. It remains a puzzle.

page *see* **on the same page**

paper

The word arrived in English from French in the fourteenth century, and sometimes spelled *papyr*, echoing its origin in Latin and Greek *papyrus*, the tall flowering plant that grew in the valley of the River Nile, used by the Ancient Egyptians as a source of writing material. Its everyday sense has given rise to several idioms. The oldest, from early in the sixteenth century, is 'set pen to paper' – these days, more usually 'put pen to paper' – meaning to start writing about something. It has remained in use, even in the digital age, and I've seen it in several online guides to writing on the internet. But not everyone is comfortable with it, and there's been a search for a more appropriate alternative. The front runner seems to be 'put fingers to keyboard'.

Later in the sixteenth century we find the very common 'on paper', less often 'upon paper', with the core meaning of 'in writing' or 'in print'. What's interesting is the way that this expression very quickly took on a non-literal meaning. To say that a recommendation was 'on paper' meant that it was a statement of principle, rather than something that would work in reality. Thomas Carlyle later summed it up well, in *Sartor Resartus: The Life and Opinions of Herr Teufelsdrockh* (1836), when his professorial narrator comments: 'How beautiful to die of broken-heart, on Paper! Quite another thing in practice.' And it's this sense of 'failing to live up to expectations' that is the dominant meaning nowadays. Nor does 'on paper' necessarily mean that the plan or promise should be written down. When people say that something 'sounds good on paper', all they mean is 'in theory'.

The nineteenth century also produced a further idiom: 'not worth the paper it's written on', meaning that some proposal is of little (or no) value. My favourite example here is a playful adaptation by the film producer Samuel Goldwyn, well known for his cheeky quips: 'An oral agreement isn't worth the paper it's written on.'

pen

The word has persisted, despite many changes in writing technology. It was originally borrowed from Latin *penna* in Anglo-Saxon times, and given a fresh boost from French *penne* in the Middle Ages. For centuries it was a writing implement that used ink, first with the sharpened end of a feather (a 'quill pen'), then with a metal tip ('nib') fitted into a holder, and then with the holder containing its own supply of ink (as in a 'fountain pen'). In the twentieth century we see the nib replaced by a ball (a 'ballpoint pen'), and finally in the digital age we encounter an 'electric' or 'electronic pen' for writing onto a screen, or onto a surface connected to a computer. At the same time, other adjectival words distinguished different functions, such as 'marker pen'.

Also in the Middle English period, *pen* transferred from the physical implement to the writer (as in 'there's evidence of more than one pen at work') and to the practice of writing. In the mid-fourteenth century the translator John Trevisa wrote of Julius Caesar that (in modern spelling) 'his hand was able to the pen as to the sword'. That theme was taken up by many writers, such as William Cobbett, who observed in his *A Grammar of the English Language* (1818) that 'Tyranny has no enemy so formidable as the pen'. A present-day idiom soon followed, with Edward Bulwer-Lytton writing in his play *Richelieu* (1839) that 'Beneath the rule of men entirely great / The pen is mightier than the sword.'

We'd expect such an everyday word to be the source of many idioms, but in fact it generated very few. We find 'touch the pen' from the sixteenth century – the practice of an illiterate person touching the pen of someone signing their name on their behalf, thereby giving authority to the signature. That transmuted into a meaning of authentication, without any physical act: 'I never touched the pen', someone might say, surprised at seeing their name listed under a petition. 'Poison pen' arrived in the nineteenth century, describing anonymous abusive letters. Lexicographer Eric Partridge found a few more uses in that century, such as the slang description of male impotence: he has 'no more ink in his pen'. And it was picked up by cockneys as part of rhyming slang: 'pen and ink'? Stink.

Sometime during the twentieth century we find this advice for men: 'don't dip your pen in the company's ink', meaning that one should avoid romantic relationships in the workplace. It's rarely heard these days, as the technology is dated, but there's been quite a debate online about finding a replacement. Suggestions include: 'Don't put your USB drive in your work computer', 'Don't log in to the company's wifi', 'Don't slip your dongle into your co-worker's port'. Make your choice.

pencil

The word is from French *pincel*, meaning 'a small paint brush', and this is how it was first used when it came into English in the fourteenth century: the brush had hair tapered to a point, making it suitable for painting fine details. The French word is from Latin *peniculus* 'brush', which in turn comes from the word for 'tail', *penis* – and, unsurprisingly, *pencil* became vulgar slang for the male member in the early twentieth century, and probably has a longer unrecorded history.

The modern sense – a pointed, encased stick of black metal (typically graphite) used for writing or drawing – emerged after large deposits of a black ore were discovered at Borrowdale in Cumbria in 1564. People thought the ore was lead, so early pencils came to be described as *black lead*, and later as *lead pencils* – even though there's no lead in them at all. *Graphite* entered the language a century later. Despite its popularity, relatively few idiomatic or extended uses have emerged. To 'pencil in' is the chief idiom, used since the end of the nineteenth century when making a provisional note, or a tentative arrangement. And the main extended use, from around the same time, moved away from writing on paper: facial make-up implements, such as 'eyebrow pencil' and 'lip pencil'.

Also in the nineteenth century, blue pencils came to be used by editors to make cuts or corrections in submitted material, and the practice came to be widely used for marking errors or comments in other areas, such as in schoolwork, or deleting passages, such as in a script or a legal document. As a result, the verb 'to blue-pencil' began to take on the sense of 'something unwanted' or 'censored', and to be used outside of writing. 'I'm blue-pencilling that idea', someone might say. 'To red-pencil' had a similar use, though it also had a positive role: to highlight an interesting piece of text.

Why blue? This colour was found to be useful because it wouldn't be seen when a text was photographically reproduced. The 'non-photo blue pencil' came to be an especial favourite of designers or animators sketching out a drawing before overlaying the marks with a permanent medium, such as ink.

poison pen *see* **pen**

proof

I wouldn't have included this word in a book of 'everyday' expressions a few years ago, but times have changed, and the internet has brought it into the public domain. There are dozens of sites now offering proofreading tools and services, and the growing popularity of self-publishing is making the notion a routine encounter for many. One of its functions has been around since the early days of the internet: spellcheckers. But, as we all know, these aren't perfect, as they will miss homonyms such as *plane* for *plain*, so nothing beats the need for a careful, thorough, letter-by-letter reading of a text before publishing it.

Proof came into English from French in the early Middle Ages, in a plethora of meanings all to do with trials and testing. We still do use it in this way, especially in the idiom *the proof of the pudding* – a shortened form of a proverb first recorded by the historian William Camden in 1605: 'All the proof of a pudding is in the eating.' Its use in printing was probably there as soon as that technology arrived in the fifteenth century, but no recorded use of the term in that context has so far been discovered before 1602. The related terms – *to proofread, proofreading* and *proofreader* – are all much later, during the nineteenth century.

The websites need to be used cautiously. Most say they are there to 'improve' your writing. But many are really pedantic, and warn you against usages that are actually perfectly normal. I put a prepared piece of my own writing into a couple, to test them, and was firmly told off for using passives, splitting an infinitive, beginning a sentence with *and*, and ending one with a preposition. And I thought the old prescriptivism was dead. It's evidently gained new life online.

Ps and Qs

Why these two letters should have prompted an array of idioms is a mystery, but there have been many theories. The earliest usage so far recorded dates from the early seventeenth century, where 'to be P and Q' meant to be of top quality, and 'to be on one's Ps and Qs' was to be on one's best behaviour or to be alert. These seem to have died out, but they've been replaced by an eighteenth-century expression: 'mind (or watch) one's Ps and Qs'. If someone tells you this, they're suggesting you need to be careful about how you behave or how you speak. Mind your manners! People weren't sure how to spell it. We see 'pees and cues' and 'peas and cues'.

Other meanings emerged in that century. To 'know your Ps and Qs' could literally mean a knowledge of the alphabet, and how to spell, or more generally to know your way around a subject, or to be aware of the rules of etiquette. 'Forgetting your Ps and Qs' would be a social disaster. In the nineteenth century the pedagogical sense developed, 'to learn your Ps and Qs', and this has led to the most popular suggestion about the origin of the expression – that it was the result of children having difficulty distinguishing lower case p and q when learning to read and write. Typesetters, in the days of manual printing, faced the same problem when selecting the letters from their case box, and putting them (back to front) in the right place.

The common belief that it's a shortened form of 'pleases and thank-yous' has to be ruled out, as that expression isn't attested until the twentieth century. But no explanation accounts satisfactorily for all the meanings. I rather like the child-based theory, and also the proposal that the expression began in taverns, with landlords confusing pints and quarts of beer when they wrote out a bill for a customer. Highly plausible, especially if the innkeeper had 'had a few'.

publish

This word arrived from Latin *publicare* via French in the fourteenth century, and was immediately used in its source meanings, such as 'make public' and 'make generally known', as well as in relation to the publication of books and documents. It's a word that resisted idiomatic exploitation, but everything changed in 1824, when Arthur Wellesley, the first Duke of Wellington, received a threat by a publisher to make public his relationship with a well-known courtesan in a 'kiss and tell' memoir. The story goes that Wellington's reply was 'Publish and be damned!' The liaison was indeed published, but if it did harm his reputation, it didn't stop him becoming prime minister four years later.

The riposte was never forgotten, and in the twentieth century seemed to capture a mood of confident self-expression: 'I don't care what you think.' It was chosen as the name of an independent publishing fair between 2004 and 2013 in London, which showcased books from outside the mainstream, including self-publishing. And it had an earlier history in relation to a national newspaper. In 1953 Hugh Cudlipp called his book *Publish and be Damned*, subtitled *The Astonishing Story of the Daily Mirror* – the thrust being that this was a paper ready to stand up to the establishment in representing the concerns of ordinary people. But that message turned sour when illegal snooping became part of the story, and some sixty years later the *Press Gazette* ran a piece with the headline 'How publish and be damned took on a new meaning at the Mirror'.

Several other books and articles have used the expression as their title, including in the academic world, where the mantra of 'publish or perish', referring to the success of an academic's career, has attracted the variation 'Publish or be Damned'. And it has had a boost from the internet, where the belief that people can publish anything they like, especially in social media, has been challenged in the courts. As a law blog put it in 2017: 'Publish and be damned: the old adage applies equally to internet users.'

put pen to paper *see* **paper**

read (something)

Telling someone to 'read' begins several twentieth-century idioms, often starting life in American English. One of the most famous is 'read my lips'. This had a literal meaning in the nineteenth century, referring to a deaf person's ability to understand someone who is speaking by reading their lips. But it later came to be used as an imperative meaning 'listen carefully to what I'm saying', with an implication of 'take me at my word'. The fame stems from its use by President George H.W. Bush, who used it in his speech to the 1988 Republican National Convention: 'Read my lips: no new taxes.'

Around the same time we find 'read the room' in public-speaking situations, meaning to be aware of the mood or behaviour of an audience. It attracted many new users when chat rooms arrived. And when podcasts and blogs use it, the reference is to a strange notion of 'room' – the hoped-for online readership. I've heard it used domestically too, referring to the emotional atmosphere in the rooms of a house.

Earlier in the century, a fascinating use came out of American card gambling. If you had a winning poker hand, you could express your satisfaction with a neat dig at your opponent, as you display your cards: 'read 'em and weep!' Dice gambling attracted its use too. And you could say it for other situations, such as drawing attention (often in a jocular way) to a news item that you know is dear to your listener's heart: 'read it and weep!'

Reading has always attracted idiomatic usage, as we'll see again in the next entries. In the seventeenth century if you 'read someone a lesson' or 'a lecture', you were giving them a reprimand. And in the nineteenth if you 'took something as read', you'd be taking a point for granted, not needing any justification or discussion. We've seen what happened in the twentieth. Doubtless the internet will generate even more idioms in the twenty-first.

read between the lines

The 'lines' in a piece of writing – rows of letters, punctuation marks and spaces – have been so-named since Anglo-Saxon times. The word is an application of the general notions of a string of things, a cord, a linear mark, and several other senses all ultimately derived from Latin *linea*, which meant 'a linen thread'. It was hugely fruitful, adopted in virtually all areas of knowledge, as the parenthetical examples suggest in such domains as music (lines of a stave), mathematics (geometrical lines), travel (railway lines), commerce (product lines), biology (lineage), communications (phone lines) and programming (lines of code). It's surprising, then, to find so few idioms making use of the word.

In the world of books, there's really only one that's achieved any presence: 'reading between the lines' – to discover a meaning in a text that is implied but not actually stated in the words. It may be to do with factual content, the writer's intentions or feelings, or any other kind of inference. It became popular in the mid-nineteenth century, and since then has been adopted – and often adapted – in a variety of settings. It's especially popular in music, where it's been chosen as the name of over a dozen songs or albums. Crime writers love it.

So do railway enthusiasts, because of the obvious pun: for instance, it's the title of the newsletter of Lancashire's Community Railways group.

But the best puns (or worst, depending on your point of view) are those based on the existence of the town in Berkshire, Reading. (For those outside the UK who may not know, this is pronounced *red*-ing. It was founded by an Anglo-Saxon chief. The name means 'the people of Reada'.) It's the former name of a local theatre company. And it was the title of a book about the town's football club, after its best season ever, when it won promotion to the top league in 2007: *Reading Between the Lines: A Season of Dreams*. (As a former professor of linguistics at Reading University, and a fan, I have to add that, as I write, the pun no longer works, after two relegations and another just avoided. Or, if it does, the subtitle would have to be *A Season of Nightmares*.)

read someone like a book *see* **book: speaking, reading & writing**

read the riot act

It's amazing that a small piece of government legislation should still be in the popular mind, despite it having fallen out of use and ultimately being superseded; but that is what happened to this expression. It all began in 1714, after a period of civil unrest in Britain. The Riot Act came into force the following year. It begins:

> Whereas of late many rebellious riots and tumults
> have been in divers parts of this kingdom,
> to the disturbance of the publick peace, and
> the endangering of his Majesty's person and
> government...

and it goes on to state the criteria:

> if any persons to the number of twelve or more,
> being unlawfully, riotously, and tumultuously
> assembled together, to the disturbance of the
> publick peace ... such assembly shall be, by
> proclamation to be made in the King's name,
> in the form herin after directed, to disperse
> themselves.

They had an hour to do it, otherwise they would be 'adjudged felons, and shall suffer death as in a case of felony without benefit of clergy'. This is what you would hear, if you were one of the rioters:

> Our sovereign Lord the King chargeth and
> commandeth all persons, being assembled,
> immediately to disperse themselves, and peaceably
> to depart to their habitations, or to their lawful
> business, upon the pains contained in the
> act made in the first year of King George, for
> preventing tumults and riotous assemblies. God
> save the King.

Seventy years later we see it being used, without capital letters, as a strong warning to anyone causing a commotion, and especially to noisy or disobedient children. An institution could be reprimanded too: someone might say they're going to read the riot act to an organization, or even a country, as in this headline from the *Telegraph* in 2023: 'US reads "riot act" to Germany over refusal to send Leopard tanks to Ukraine.'

Why was the idiom so successful? The alliteration and rhythm in the phrase must have helped. 'If you don't shut up I'll read you the public order act of 1986' doesn't quite have the same ring, somehow.

reams

Arabic *rizma* is the original source of this word, meaning a bale or bundle of some kind, including paper; and when it eventually arrived in English in the fourteenth century, via French or Dutch, that was its application. To begin with, it was given a precise quantification: a 'ream' was a specific number of sheets of printing paper. But during the fifteenth century it began to be used in the plural to mean a large quantity of paper, without saying exactly how much. People would talk about 'reams of correspondence', or making 'reams of notes'.

It was a short step from here, in the seventeenth century, for it to mean a large quantity of anything – poetry, roses, people... It could also apply to speech: reams of arguments, abuse, chit-chat... But the most unexpected use was to find it in the world of horse racing, where names from the book world are few and far between. In the 1990s Reams of Verse was a regular winner, including The Oaks in 1997. More recently, Reams of Love has also done quite well. Punters take note: horses with book-world names could be worth backing.

red-letter day

This expression originally referred to the convention of identifying a special day in a calendar or an almanac by writing its date and name in the colour red. The practice is known from classical Roman times, and was adopted in the Christian era to identify important festivals and saints' feast days. Other days were written or printed in black: 'black-letter days'. It is first recorded in English in the seventeenth century, and by the nineteenth its use had extended to mean any memorable or significant day, or a day perceived to be one of good fortune. The black-letter days showed a similar development: these were days thought to be inauspicious or best forgotten because of some unhappy event.

The English High Court gave the expression a technical application. For judges, red-letter days are a set of saints' days and national celebrations, especially connected with the royal family. On such days, if they are sitting in a law court, they wear scarlet robes.

Letter turns up in another legal-inspired idiom: 'the letter of the law', recorded since the sixteenth century. In its popular use it isn't restricted to laws, but applies to any rules or regulations in any field. If we follow 'the letter of the law', we respect the exact meaning as expressed in the words. The contrast is with 'the spirit of the law', where we prioritize the intention lying behind the words. 'To the letter' is similar: if I 'obey you to the letter', I mean I'll do what you say exactly, to the fullest extent.

royalty

It may seem a long way from monarchy to the use of this word in the world of books, but the connection is logical enough. It arrived in English from French, along with *royal*, in the fifteenth century, and almost immediately developed the sense of a monarch's rights and privileges. In Act 2 of Shakespeare's *Richard II*, Bolingbroke bemoans the way his 'rights and royalties' have been taken away from him. A financial perspective isn't far away.

By the nineteenth century the term had narrowed to mean payments made to people in various industries, such as to a landowner for mining rights, or to the owner of a technical process. In the 1850s we see its use in relation to book publishing: the agreed percentage of revenue from each copy sold, paid to the writer. The procedure wasn't restricted to books. It was used in relation to profits from musical performance, becoming more widely known after the arrival of broadcasting. I wasn't sure just how far the word had become part of everyday consciousness until I heard someone say 'Yes, you can borrow my wheelie bin, but you'll have to pay me royalties.'

rubber stamp

When this device came into use, in the later decades of the nineteenth century, it had a double meaning. It referred both to the handheld device itself, with a text or a design cut into a flat piece of rubber, and to the imprinted message this produced, the result of inking the stamp and pressing it onto a surface. It began life in the world of documents, where it signalled an endorsement, authorization or other official sanction. But its convenient size soon led to its use in a wide range of settings, such as photography, textiles, food packaging and the visual arts.

The expression was a noun and a verb, and both motivated idiomatic usage in the early part of the twentieth century. The verb was especially popular, referring to cases where an individual, a group or an organization endorsed a text or a course of action routinely or in an automatic way, without paying attention to what was involved. It was usually negative in tone, as it still is: to say that a committee has 'rubber-stamped the decision' means that they haven't considered it carefully, even though they have the power to do so. Of all the citations that the *Oxford English Dictionary* has collected to illustrate this use, I like this one best, from a letter written to the *Radio Times* in 1973: 'I'd written a fan letter to Bing Crosby... I received a photo of him back – with his autograph rubber-stamped across it.'

rubric

This is a word many people never come across, other than in certain settings where it's common. It began life in Roman times, when red ochre (*rubrica* in Latin) was used to highlight the chapter headings in certain books. After it arrived in English, via French, in the fourteenth century, the practice transferred to religious settings, identifying the initial capital letters or headings in a liturgical text, along with the directions for carrying out an order of service – a convention still widely used today.

By the eighteenth century it had widened its meaning to include any set of rules or prescriptions.

We see such expressions as 'a rubric of conduct' and a 'new rubric' (replacing an old one). Essentially, the term had come to mean an established custom. At the same time, it retained specialized senses in law and religion.

It's in the world of education that most people encounter the term. I still recall the repeated advice of my teachers in secondary school to 'read the rubric' at the top of an examination paper, to make sure I answered the questions correctly. And in the USA it refers to a type of scoring guide for grading assignments, typically tabular in form: it identifies the specific requirements and components involved, and provides feedback to students.

Despite its somewhat arcane tone, *rubric* has proved attractive as a company name – over forty firms registered in the UK, for instance. Most of them offer management or consulting services of some kind, but the fields are wide-ranging, including health, law, translation and communications. There are even acronyms. Regional Universities Building Research Infrastructure Collaboratively. Or, if you prefer: Reliability Usability Behaviour Reflection Information and Creativity.

schedule

There are always two sides to etymology: the history of the meaning and the history of the form. Most of the entries in this book focus on the meaning; but for this word I find the story of the form just as interesting. It came into English from French in the fourteenth century, with an earlier history in Latin, where it was the diminutive of *sceda*, meaning 'a little piece of paper'. The Romans got it from the Greeks, where the source word meant 'a papyrus leaf'.

When it first arrived, *schedule* kept that diminutive sense: it referred to a slip of paper, a small piece or scroll of parchment, or something similar, such as a label or a ticket. But by the seventeenth century it was being used for longer documents, sometimes simply containing information, sometimes long lists, inventories or tables, especially with the text arranged under formal headings. Shakespeare uses the word in both ways. When in Act 3 of *Julius Caesar* Artemidorus tells Caesar to 'Read this schedule', he means no more than what's written on his sheet or scroll of paper; but when in Act 1 of *Twelfth Night* Olivia tells the disguised Viola that she will 'give out divers [several] schedules of my beauty', she means a listing. As she goes on to say: 'It shall be inventoried.'

The French form was *cedule*, beginning with [s], and that's how it was pronounced in English – a pronunciation that stayed right until the nineteenth century. The first spellings were *cedule* and *sedule*, but the Latin spelling proved influential, and so we then find *scedule*, *schedule* and *shedule*, among several other variants. It's surprising that those spellings didn't influence pronunciation sooner, but eventually the [sh] sound became the norm, with a [sk] alternative reflecting the sound of the original Greek word.

The stage was set for the present-day transatlantic divide, with 'shed-' beginning the word in British English and 'sked-' beginning it in American English. But times change, and the American form has steadily increased its reach. I was brought up to say 'shed-', but my children all say 'sked-', and so when talking to them I find myself slipping into 'sked-' too. 'Shed-' may not have long to live.

shut *or* close the books

At first this expression was about real books – the account books of a business. At the end of a financial year, or some other fiscal period, no further entries would be allowed. The books would be 'shut' or 'closed' until a new period began, so that the accounts could be balanced. Sometimes it meant that a business had closed down. The expression entered English towards the end of the seventeenth century, and a hundred years later we find a figurative development in which the closing affects someone or something. There are two linguistic differences: the expression is followed by *on*, and we see a singular *book* as well as a plural. 'It's time to shut the book(s) on the affair.'

As that example suggests, the core meaning of the new usage is 'finish an activity' or 'draw a line under a situation', usually one that's been causing problems, upset or embarrassment. A decision is made not to waste any more time or energy by trying to deal with it or talking about it. The matter is closed. What follows the *on* can be anything – a person, a place, an event, a policy, a scandal, a relationship...

Headline-writers love it. 'Close the Book on Literary Exports' headed a *Guardian* article about the extent to which the manuscripts of British authors end up in foreign (and especially American) libraries. A reporter for the *Wall Street Journal* visited a college library and saw more computers than books: 'Don't Close the Book on Books' said the header. And a website on how to ensure a successful retirement extended the idiom: 'Don't close the book when you can start a new chapter' – or, in my case, write a book for the Bodleian.

sign on the dotted line

Dotted lines began to appear on documents in the seventeenth century, with various functions. A linear sequence of dots – or dashes – could represent such features as a route on a map, a direction of flow in an anatomy drawing, a boundary around an image, or could simply offer a contrast with a continuous line in a diagram. But in a document it would delimit a space for a signature; and the present-day idiom stems from that. We begin to see it used in the early twentieth century, especially for formal documents, such as contracts. By 'signing on the dotted line', signers show that they accept the terms stated in the document. An extended use soon followed. Anyone agreeing to something or making a firm commitment could be said to 'sign on the dotted line', even though there might be no actual dotted line, or indeed nothing written at all. When a news report says that two countries have 'signed on the dotted line', it can simply mean they've reached an agreement.

There have been a few new uses. In the American business world, an adverbial usage emerged in the 1980s: 'to report dotted line' to someone. It's a relationship where employees report to an intermediary rather than (or as well as) to their official boss. And the digital age has brought new perspectives. A BBC news report in September 2003 brought me up short: 'Mice sign on the dotted line'. Are they really so clever? But the gloss explained all: 'Soon the way you use your mouse could help prove who you are.' It appears that scientists had found a way for people to sign their name online using a mouse instead of a pen, and that the way they moved their mouse could be a unique identifier.

Does the idiom have a future? Possibly not, according to this headline in the *Telegraph* in August 2018: 'The end of signing on the dotted line? E-signatures are as valid as paper ones, Law Commission says.'

singing from the same hymn sheet
see **on the same page**

slip

It's from Dutch or German *slippe*, a word with quite a wide range of meanings, such as 'cut', 'slit', 'strip' and 'skirt'. It entered English in the fifteenth century with the general sense of 'something small and thin', initially a shoot or cutting from a plant or tree. It then transferred to people: a child could be described as a 'slip' from its parents; and by the sixteenth century it was being widely used to refer to any young slender person, especially female – 'a slip of a girl, woman, daughter...' – though we do find 'slip of a boy' also. A range of special uses followed, expressing such notions as a strip of material, a woman's undergarment, or a narrow piece of land.

Then, as the seventeenth century approached, it began to be used in relation to paper. In printing it meant a proof on a long strip of paper – what would later be called a 'galley proof'. And, generally, any piece of paper or parchment that was long and narrow would attract the word. We find 'slip of paper' frequently used, as well as more specialized senses, such as a 'betting slip' and a 'compliment slip'. It achieved real fame in lexicography, where the citations that provide the meat of a dictionary entry were written out on 'slips'. There are famous pictures of boxes and shelves containing thousands of slips in the office of the first editor of the *Oxford English Dictionary*, Sir James Murray.

slush

There's no known source for this word, which makes me think it has to be a sound imitation, like *splash*. It's first recorded in the seventeenth century referring to partly melted snow or ice, and anyone who has walked through slush knows the hissing sound it makes. It was also used for liquid mud. So it's not surprising to find it being used in a variety of settings with a negative meaning, and publishing is one of them. In the nineteenth century it became a dismissive label for any writing thought to be overly sentimental – in effect, rubbish, drivel. It was even used as an exclamation: 'Oh slush!'

In publishing it became famous – or, rather, infamous – in the expression 'slush pile', which makes its appearance in the early twentieth century. It referred to all the unsolicited manuscripts sent to a publishing house by aspiring authors, such as book proposals, drafts of whole books, and magazine articles. Not everyone in publishing liked the term, as it suggested everything in the pile was going to be equally rubbish, which was patently not the case, for some success stories came out of it. And it showed little respect for the enthusiasm and commitment that the putative authors were displaying. However, the size of the pile was usually considerable, by all accounts – often several thousand in a year – and as the quality of submissions was often very low the term has stayed in use in the publishing world, and achieved a certain amount of use outside it, referring to any informal collection of magazines, newspapers or other literature. I know one academic who calls the pile of not-yet-read journals in his office his slush pile. I have one myself. ☹

Self-publishing online, along with submission management software, has changed the situation to some extent, though it may just be that the centre of gravity of the slush pile has shifted. As one online writer put it, 'Is the Kindle the new slush-pile?'

small print *see* **fine print**
something to write home about *see* **writing**
speak like a book *see* **book: speaking, reading & writing**

speak volumes

This story begins with the Latin verb *volvere*, meaning 'to roll'. From it came the noun *volumen*, meaning a roll, scroll or other circular object, such as a coil or a wreath. It came into English in the fourteenth century in the sense of a roll of writing material, such as parchment, as well as the work written on it. Then it extended to the collection of sheets of paper bound up to make a book, and we see the modern meaning beginning to appear. By the sixteenth century the 'book' sense had become the dominant one, with *volume* suggesting works of special significance or size. The Bible, for example, was often called 'the sacred volume'. And then we find it used for the separately bound units of a large work: 'volume 1, 2', and so on. That led to the word moving in a fresh direction, expressing the sense of bulk or quantity: from the seventeenth century we find it referring to amounts, such as a quantity of material or sound, and these days internet traffic.

Extended uses all come from an analogy with books or quantities. In Shakespeare we find 'a volume of farewells', 'volumes of report' and 'by the volume', meaning something done a large number of times. Then, in the nineteenth century, we see 'to speak volumes' – sometimes with other verbs, such as 'tell' or 'express' – referring to gestures or facial expressions ('She gave me a look that spoke volumes') and also to any action or set of circumstances where a clear meaning is conveyed without necessarily using any words. 'Speak' has its broadest possible application here, including written language and saying nothing at all. 'His silence spoke volumes.' And an online company heads its post: 'Your emails speak volumes about your company.'

stationer

In Latin this was a *stationarius*, a 'bookseller', and when this word came into English in the fourteenth century that was how it was chiefly used, though sometimes also applied to printers and bookbinders. This uncertainty continued into the seventeenth century, where it is variously used for a publisher, a bookseller and a shop selling writing or office equipment. By the following century there was a related noun, *stationery*, meaning the articles sold by a stationer, which in modern times for most people has meant simply paper and envelopes.

The word is of particular interest to students of literary history, because there was a guild of stationers, which in the sixteenth century was given a monopoly in printing and the task of registering all books produced in England. When questions arise about the publication of plays and other works during the period, it's the Stationers' Register that is a first port of call. In it we find, for example, the earliest mention of Shakespeare's name, on 23 August 1600, when two plays were registered:

> Two bookes, the one called Muche a Doo about nothinge. Th other the second parte of the history of kinge HENRY the iiij[th] with the humours of Sir JOHN FFALLSTAFF: Wrytten by master SHAKESPERE

There is still a Worshipful Company of Stationers and Newspaper Makers, but its remit is now much broader than the above trades, including people working in photography, advertising, broadcasting, film production and digital media.

That might have been the end of the story, but for a spelling problem. A different word, *stationary* – from the same Latin source – had also come into English in the Middle Ages, and by the seventeenth century had developed the meaning of 'absence of motion' – an echo of one of the first senses of *station* as 'a fixed place'. The trouble was that this *-ary* spelling was also used for the book-world sense, and the spelling confusion has been with us ever since. So, for those still confused, a useful mnemonic is to think of *letter*, which has *e*, so it's *stationery*, whereas *car* has *a*, so it's *stationary*.

stereotype

We actually have an identifiable point of origin for this word. In the 1798 *Annual Register*, a review of history, politics and literature, there's a report about 'a new discovery in printing, which they term stereotype' – the 'they' referring to the French printer Firmin Didot and his colleague Louis-Étienne Herhan. The word comes from Greek *stereos* 'solid' + *typos* 'impression, figure', the solidity referring to the metal plate of type that was used to print pages, by contrast with the method of printing them with movable type. The cheap editions that came from this invention revolutionized the book trade in France, and beyond.

Fifty years later we find *stereotype* being used outside the printing world. It described anything being repeated without change, such as a constantly encountered form of words – what today we'd call a cliché. This meaning extended further in the early twentieth century, referring to ideas and beliefs that have become widespread in society, or oversimplified beliefs that don't correspond to factual reality. It was particularly used for the characteristics of people perceived to represent a group, reflecting the expectations, attitudes or prejudices of the user. The adjectives *stereotyped* and *stereotypical* emerged around the same time, along with the noun *stereotyping*.

Although stereotypes can be positive, they are most frequently used these days in negative contexts, identifying false or unfair characterizations of people based on such attributes as gender, ethnicity, age and regional background, and ignoring individual differences. In language study, accents are often singled out as a particularly sensitive feature that attracts stereotyped judgements, both positive (such as trustworthiness, friendliness) and negative (such as stupidity, naivety). Accents always seem to attract media headlines. 'What does your accent say about you?' turns up quite a lot – stereotypically, one might say.

stop press

Imperative verbs tend to be avoided in idioms, perhaps because people don't take kindly to being told what to do. But there are exceptions, as seen with *read by lip*s and *never judge a book by its cover*. This one is different, as it has changed its impact from being a command to being an exclamation.

It began in the early nineteenth century when a growing number of newspapers were being printed. In London alone in 1800 there were four main daily papers: *The Times*, the *Morning Post*, the *Morning Chronicle* and the *Morning Herald*, and competition was intense, with each striving to be the one with the latest news. *Stop press*, or *stop the press*, first recorded in 1807, rang out in houses when the printing of a particular issue had begun, and the editors decided to include a major piece of incoming news. Before long they hit on a more convenient strategy: to have any last-minute updates included in a separate space, headed *Stop Press*, on the front or the back page, inserted either just before or after the printing started. It became a noun: 'something's come in for the stop press'.

The news item had to be really important, as it was an expensive business to interfere with the printing process in this way, and this was evidently what gave it a general appeal, chiefly in Britain. By the end of the century it was being used idiomatically with exclamatory force to herald a piece of significant information. 'Stop press! I've got the job!' And the sense of drama and urgency proved attractive in several other settings. An Australian board game in the 1980s was called Stop Press, with the strapline 'the sizzling headline game'; and *Stop the Press* named a comedy news quiz on BBC Scotland in 2017–18. Writers began to play with it. 'Stop the Press' was the title of a 2007 article about proposed changes to censorship laws. And the wheel turned full circle when the phrase began to headline articles about the demise of a printer or a newspaper. The *Financial Times* in March 2022 was one: 'Stop press: end of an era as the FT's own printing site closes.'

take a page from someone's book

This idiom emerged towards the end of the nineteenth century, and quickly became very popular. It had various forms. Some preferred 'borrow a page…'; 'leaf' was sometimes used instead of 'page';

'out of' often replaced 'from'; and in the United States 'book' was commonly replaced by 'playbook'. That word confused the British, who thought it meant 'a book containing plays', and couldn't work out why. What they didn't realize was its source in American football, where a 'play' was a planned set of strategic actions, and the manual listing these was known as the 'playbook'.

All versions have the same aim: to copy someone's behaviour, to follow their example, to use their tactics. The relationship between the two elements is sometimes fairly obvious. An online arts site in 2023 was headed 'Young Musicians Take a Page from the Pros'. It's more interesting when the relationship makes you stop and think. 'Math Teachers Take a Page from English/Language Arts' made me wonder: how? The article (in *Education Week* during September 2019) explains: using comic books to explain mathematical concepts. And this next one was challenging. It was an opinion piece for ABC News in May 2020: 'America's COVID-19 response should borrow a page from NASA'. The key here was the recommendation to use a centralized 'Mission Control'.

And if people don't 'borrow' a page, they might 'turn the page' or 'turn a new page', an idiom that appeared at around the same time. It means 'make a fresh start'. The implication is usually negative: someone has been living through a difficult period, and now there's the prospect of a new beginning. It's time to move on.

take as gospel

The word was *god-spell* in Old English, probably most widely recognized today in the title of the 1973 film musical *Godspell*. Ask anybody what the first part of the word meant, and they will probably say 'God'. In fact it was originally the Anglo-Saxons' word for 'good', pronounced with a long vowel, [gohd]. The second part, *spell*, meant a story or saying, or speech in general. So *gospel* meant 'good tidings'. But the ambiguity of the form *god* in writing soon led to it being interpreted as the 'god story'.

In a solidly Christian era, the truth of the gospel was unquestioned, so it's not surprising to find the word being used in non-biblical contexts, especially in the idiom 'take something as/for gospel', recorded from the thirteenth century. It was used for any statement thought to be as true as the gospel. It also had a negative form: 'don't take that for gospel', meaning 'I can't vouch for its truth.'

A related idiom with even stronger force is recorded in the seventeenth century: 'the gospel truth'. This was used for any utterance thought to be unquestionably true, though over time it weakened, becoming more a colloquial affirmation of the strength of a speaker's feelings.

Religious idioms turn up in the strangest places. One of them was in the 1997 Disney animated feature film *Hercules*. The opening song is set in a museum where five female Muses come alive to sing the story, in an exuberant 'gospel' style, of how Zeus 'tamed the globe', using his thunderbolt to bring order out of chaos. The final verse gives the clue to the song's title:

> On Mt Olympus, life was neat, and smooth
>   as sweet vermouth
> Ah! Though, honey, it may seem impossible
> That's the gospel truth.

The piece is known by those last three words.

the letter of the law *see* **red-letter day**
the pen is mightier than the sword *see* **pen**
the writing on the wall *see* **writing**

throw the book at someone

Here, the 'book' is a real or imaginary listing of all the crimes or punishments recognized in a jurisdiction. It's first found in American writing from the early twentieth century, but soon broadened its reach, as so many US expressions of the time did. If accused people have the 'book thrown at' them, they are being charged with every possible offence relating to their crime. It's a rhetorical usage, meaning they'll be punished 'as severely as possible'.

One of the best illustrations I've found is in a satirical context, in Joseph Heller's 1962 novel *Catch-22*. Clevinger is one of the officers at the American base, and he gets into trouble:

> One day he had stumbled while marching to class; the next day he was formally charged with 'breaking ranks while in formation, felonious assault, indiscriminate behavior, mopery, high treason, provoking, being a smart guy, listening to classical music and so on'. In short, they threw the book at him.

A related idiom, not so widely known, is to *get* or *do the book*, meaning 'receive the maximum term of imprisonment for a crime'. But in many modern uses the thrust of the expression is against perceived failings or faults, rather than crimes. We see such headlines as 'workers throw the book at employer over pay'. One I found especially interesting was from Citizens Advice in 2014: 'Government must "throw the book" at predatory parking firms.' The inverted commas are unusual, suggesting that the writer wasn't sure if the readership would understand that this was an idiom – strange for a usage a century old.

Also in the domain of the law is the familiar 'You're booked', where a police officer (or a sports referee) takes down the personal details of someone suspected of an offence, or seen to have committed one. That use is much older, from the eighteenth century, and the general sense of *book* meaning 'enter something in a book' goes back to the Middle Ages. My favourite example here is a piece of railway workers' slang from the early twentieth century. It's a warning about not walking on a line where you'd be facing certain death if a train came along: you'd be 'booked for kingdom come'!

tittle *see* **jot**
to the letter *see* **red-letter day**
touch the pen *see* **pen**
turn the page *see* **take a page from someone's book**

turn-up for the books

Here the 'books' are the notebooks used by bookmakers at horse-racing meetings, in which they would write down the bets people made. Every now and then there would be a horse that nobody expected would do well, so nobody backed it. As a consequence, if it won it would be a surprise – and a pleasant one for the bookmakers, as they wouldn't have to pay out anything.

The expression is first recorded at the end of the nineteenth century, and seems to be a mainly British English usage. I remember an American visitor being puzzled by it. The notion of 'turning up' here is much older, dating from the sixteenth century. It's from card games, where the cards are placed face down, and players hope to 'turn up' a winning card, such as an ace. So the idiom developed the sense of a completely unexpected turn of events, and usually a welcome one – a stroke of luck.

It's come to be used in this way in a remarkable range of settings, nothing to do with books at all, such as a sudden burst of sunshine during a rain-filled holiday. But the attraction of the literal meaning of 'book' has given rise to an even more remarkable array of usages in literary contexts. As a noun, it headed a newspaper report about a proposal to renovate a library; as a verb, a publicity request to come to the Bologna Children's Book Fair. And sometimes the literal and the metaphorical senses combine. *Turn Up for the Books* names a BBC Sounds podcast series, glossed as 'surprising and friendly book recommendations'.

typecasting

I don't think the printers who introduced this term in the nineteenth century could ever have imagined its future use in the twentieth. For them it was simply a word describing the way pieces of type for printing (sorts) would be made by pouring molten metal into moulds shaped like the desired characters. As technology changed, the term was replaced by typesetting, but the original usage has achieved a fresh presence in computer programming, where it refers to the process of converting an expression of a given type (such as numbers, letters or strings) into another – also known as 'type conversion'.

The extended use arose in the 1920s in the world of cinema, and later in theatre and television. It came to mean giving a role to actors based on their perceived success in previous productions – a hero, tough guy, girl next door, comic fool, maternal figure, and so on. It was a concern of the actors in the *Star Trek* series, for example, that they would never be given roles other than the ones with which they were most associated – though some did eventually 'play against type'.

A surprising development is to see the label being used outside of acting. Anyone given a particular task to do can be described as typecast, if someone thinks it suits their character, or some aspect of their behaviour. Whole communities can be typecast in this way, as 'unfriendly', 'reserved', 'warm', 'loud', ... The decision might be based on a single feature, such as an accent, or a well-known personality, real or fictitious. Statements such as 'He's a typical *A*' or 'Not everyone in *B* behaves like *C*' illustrate the way typecasting can infiltrate thinking. (Replace *A* by any nationality or ethnic group, *B* by any region or country, and *C* by any well-known person.)

upper and lower case

These terms never used to have a life outside the printing and publishing industries; but since the arrival of electronic communication they've become part of the terminological stock-in-trade of computer programmers, web designers, self-publishers, bloggers, and a host of other digerati. They were introduced in the decades following the arrival of printing in England in the late sixteenth century. Printers needed a convenient means of displaying the pieces of type that their compositors would use to make up lines of print. The solution was to place the type in two shallow trays (*cases*), one above the other, located at a convenient distance near the printing press. Each case was divided into compartments containing instances of a particular item. The lower case, closer to the compositor, and so easily reached, held the frequently occurring letters, punctuation marks and spaces; the upper case, taking a little more effort to reach, held the capital letters, which were less often required.

Seventeenth-century typographers extended the terms to describe the letters themselves, and it's the distinction between large (capital) and small (minuscule) letters that's motivated a wider use of the case terminology. Large in size came to be associated with greater importance (*see* **with a capital —**), and as a consequence, during the twentieth century, especially in the USA, *lower case* came to mean 'unimportant', 'insignificant' or just 'small in size'. We find someone described as having a 'lower case moustache'; a low-ranking mafia member as a 'lower case soldier'; and in 2007 the break-up of the Switchfoot rock band led to the founding of a record label they called *lowercase people*, after their song 'Company Car'. It begins:

> Mike was right when he said; I'd put up
> A fight to be someone
> A fight to be me
> But see now I'm down
> Under the pavement
> Of capital hills and lowercase people.

So far, *uppercase* hasn't achieved such a cool presence.

vignette

The word arrived in English from French in the eighteenth century, referring to a small ornamental design on a blank space in a book or document. It became a widespread feature of nineteenth-century publications, usually appearing where there was an important transition in the content, such as at the beginning or end of a chapter. Vignettes weren't enclosed in a border, and often their edges would gradually shade off into the paper.

Once the notion was established, it was adopted in a variety of settings. By the 1880s it was being used in literature to mean a short piece of writing that could be extracted from a work, acting as a kind of teaser. It might be a description of a character or an event, and the effect was to make you want to read more. It also described a comic sketch in a music hall, and, later, the sketches in radio and television comedies. There was an academic application too: a research presentation might include a short scenario acting as a stimulus for the detailed analysis following.

Other art forms, such as music and theatre, also used vignettes, the excerpts illustrating the character of the work as a whole. Film trailers, introduced in the 1920s, had the same function. And when the video era began, it turned up in sports, such as wrestling, featuring someone who was going to appear at a forthcoming event. The visual arts used the term too. In photography it described photos with a darker or shaded edge. In stamp collecting it identified the central design, such as a monarch's head.

In recent times the term has sometimes been used for physical objects. In the area of immigration it describes the visa sticker that is attached to a passport once an application has been successful. And in some central European countries it names a method of taxing vehicles for travelling along certain roads, based on a period of time (such as a day, a week…) rather than on the distance travelled. You purchase a coloured sticker that you fix to your windscreen – and sometimes have difficulty removing, which was one of the motivations for an electronic solution, linked to your number plate. The linguistic result was an unexpected collocation: a 'digital vignette'.

volume *see* **speak volumes**

watermark

The original meaning of this word, in the sixteenth century, was a level reached by an amount of water in a container, a well or a watercourse, and the mark that this left when it lowered. The notion of a level then merged with that of a standard or norm, and this is the context needed to see its use in relation to paper. Watermarks began to be used in paper from as early as the thirteenth century in Europe. Paper mills needed a method to identify themselves and to distinguish different batches or grades of paper – a kind of early trademark. An individual design was pressed into a sheet of paper during manufacture, which could be seen only when the sheet was held up to the light. Today, watermarks are a valuable source of information about the date and provenance of an old document, as well as offering brand consistency and asset protection. They are widely used in photography.

The word didn't enter English until the early 1700s. Since then it has developed in several directions. It's been used in the sense of a motif or theme in an artistic work. Something that recurs in a body of work, such as a frequent poetic image or a particular colour, could be described as the artist's watermark. Then, in the 1990s, a computational use emerged for a piece of code invisibly embedded in a digital file, or in an audio or video recording, which provided copyright protection. A 'digital watermark'.

It proved to be an appealing image to artists, especially singers. It named the third solo album by Art Garfunkel in 1977, and the second album by Enya in 1988. It's the title of a 1987 collection of poems by Nobel Prize winner Joseph Brodsky. And it names an art gallery in Harrogate.

widows & orphans

Whoever first thought that this pair of terms had a place in the world of printing deserves a prize for innovative metaphors! *Widow* is a really ancient word, found in Old English and other Germanic languages, and with links to earlier languages in the Indo-European family, such as Welsh, where a widow is *gweddw*. *Orphan* came into English more recently, in the fifteenth century, from Latin (and earlier Greek) *orphanus*. The two words have one thing in common: the people are both alone – no husband, no parents. So it was a brilliant insight to see that they could describe two lonely phenomena in printed text. *Widow* is first recorded from the early years of the twentieth century; *orphan* some time later.

Widow describes the situation where the last word or line of a paragraph appears alone at the top of the next page. *Orphan* describes the situation where the first line of a new paragraph appears alone at the bottom of a page. Some manuals use *widow* for both, but I think the distinction is worth making, as the solutions can be very different. Pulling back one or two words from the top of a page might involve slightly rephrasing the text. Taking over a line to the next page leaves a space behind which needs to be eliminated, usually by resetting the previous lines.

Note that we're talking aesthetics here, not semantics. It's the look of the page that offends. Meaning isn't involved.

with a capital —

The blank is filled by the capital letter of whatever word precedes 'with'. So… 'I said no with a capital *N*', 'That's quality with a capital *Q*', 'He's trouble with a capital *T*', and thousands more using every letter of the alphabet. The expression always adds emphasis to the word in question, and suggests that there's something special or quintessential about it.

This formula dates from the mid-nineteenth century, but the association of capital letters with emphasis is much earlier. In the previous century we find 'speaking in capitals' for someone saying something in a particularly emphatic way. And *capital* has always had an underlying sense of 'important' or 'chief', as in 'capital cities'. It came into English probably from French in the fourteenth century, or perhaps directly from Latin, where it derives from the word for 'head', *caput*. (*Chapter* is related: *see* **chapter and verse**.)

The opposite formula also exists, though it hasn't achieved so much presence, probably because there aren't so many prompt words beginning with a capital letter. The speaker means that the behaviour is more general than the usual meaning, or not so extreme. It may even have a diminishing force. We hear such things as 'I'm conservative with a small *c*' and 'He's a saint with a small *s*.' And the focused word doesn't always have to begin with a capital. 'They're doing research with a very small *r*.'

The convention attracts the playful. 'That's cool with a capital *K*.' There's a white wine blend called 'Trouble with a Capital "Z"'. And occasionally it's the shape of the letter that is the focus. 'Look at that capital *D*' – referring to the rounded shape of a rather large belly.

write the book on it *see* **book: speaking, reading & writing**

writing

The act of writing has been a fruitful area for idiom generation. One of the earliest, in the sixteenth century, is 'written in *X*', where *X* is a noun expressing the notion of something changing or impermanent – today usually 'sand', but formerly also 'dust', 'air' and 'water'. What would be 'written in sand'? Typically promises, vows, undertakings, or the like, where it's felt that the person making the claim isn't going to honour it. The opposite would be a hard substance, such as 'marble' or 'stone'.

The seventeenth century brought 'the writing (is) on the wall' – a biblical allusion. Chapter 5 of the book of Daniel describes how, during a feast given by King Belshazzar, mysterious writing appears on a wall, which Daniel interprets to mean that the king's empire is going to be destroyed. When the idiom came into English it appeared both as a phrase and later as a sentence: 'The writing is on the wall.' Either way, it means there are clear signs that a decline in fortunes or a disaster of some sort is imminent. It seems very popular in sport. 'The writing is on the wall for...' – insert your team or sportsperson here, if things are not going so well for them.

Also in the seventeenth century we find something being 'writ large' or 'written large', referring to anything that's perfectly clear or obvious (in the view of the speaker), or on a large scale. 'Science is just common sense writ large', says one online forum. 'Is philosophy just neurosis writ large?' heads another. The opposite, 'writ small', has a contemporary presence too, usually meaning 'on a small scale'. I remember someone saying about a local

WRITING 147

beach near where I live, on a particularly hot day last summer: 'This is the Riviera writ small.'

Then in the nineteenth century we find 'written all over' someone or something. The commonest noun is 'face', referring to an expression that makes it perfectly clear how the person is feeling. The formula is 'X is written all over Y's face'. For X read 'happiness, disappointment, surprise, excitement...' For Y read 'his, her, my uncle's, Fred's...' But the idiom can also apply to things: 'the plan had failure written all over it'. Sport has picked this one up as well, when predicting outcomes: 'That match has draw written all over it.' I suppose commentators could use the 'face' idiom here as well: 'That match has draw written all over its face.' They probably do.

I've certainly heard them use another nineteenth-century one: 'that goal/shot/jump... is something to write home about', meaning it's really noteworthy, out of the ordinary. The opposite is just as popular: 'That game/pass/result... is nothing to write home about' – it's mediocre, unappealing, ordinary, average. Reviewers and critics like it when talking about a book, a taste, a performance... 'The lasagne was nothing to write home about.' Shame.

writ large, written all over, written in sand *see* **writing**

Further Reading

Brewer's Dictionary of Phrase and Fable has become so well known that it's usually referred to simply as *Brewer's*. First published in 1870, it had twenty editions by 2018. The name refers to Rev Dr Ebenezer Cobham Brewer (1810–1897), a Baptist minister, schoolteacher and writer of reference books.

The unabridged *Oxford English Dictionary*, online edition at www.oed.com. It's a subscription site, but worth every penny, for there is no equal to its historical coverage and treatment, not only of individual words, but also of derived phrases.

Eric Partridge, *A Dictionary of Slang and Unconventional English* (Routledge), first published in 1937, and updated and edited in 1984 by Paul Beale. Look up *book* in this work and you'll find a remarkable collection of usages from little-known sources, such as the way the word was used in nineteenth- and early-twentieth-century public school and armed forces slang.

Apart from these works of general reference, anyone interested in the history of English vocabulary will find more from my **pen** (see page 95) in the following titles: *The Stories of English* (2004), *Words, Words, Words* (2006), *The Story of English in 100 Words* (2011), *Words in Time and Place* (2014) and *The Cambridge Encyclopedia of the English Language* (3rd edn, 2019).

Index

agony aunt 4
agony uncle 4
anthology 5
appendix 7
back number 8
bad books, be in someone's 24
bible 10
biro 12
black books 78
black-letter day 111
blot one's copybook 13
blue pencil 98
blueprint 15
blurb 16
book, bring to 26
book, by the 28
book, every trick in the 23
book, get/do 134
book, in someone's 23
book, in the 23
book, judging by its cover 69

book, know someone like a 18
book, little black 78
book, oldest rule in the 23
book, read someone like a 18
book, speak like a 18
book, take a page from someone's 130
book, take/borrow a leaf out of someone's 72
book, talk like a 18
book, throw at someone 26, 134
book of (the) words 21
booked 135
bookend 20
book(s), for the 23
book(s), one for the 23
books, be in someone's good/bad 24
books, cook the 41
books, imagined 23

books, in the 87
books, on/off the 86
books, shut/close the 117
books, turn-up for the 136
bookworm 24
borrow a leaf/page out of someone's book 130
bright page 71
bring to book 26
bullets 27
capital (letter), with a 145
caption 29
cartoon 31
catchword 33
chapter and verse 34
cliché 36
close the books 117
closed book 90
code 38
commonplace 39
cook the books 41
copy 42
copybook, blot one's 13
cover, judging a book by its 69
dab hand 44
dark page 71
deadline 46
do the book 134
dog-eared 47
don't dip your pen in the company's ink 97
dotted line, sign on the 119
every trick in the book 23

face, written all over one's 148
fine print 49
foolscap 51
forget your Ps and Qs 101
four-letter word 52
front-page news 71
get the book 134
gloss (over) 54
good books, be in someone's 24
gospel, take as 132
gospel truth 133
graffiti 56
gutter press 60
headline 58
hit the headlines 58
hot off the press 59
hymn sheet, singing from the same 89
icon(ic) 61
impression 63
ink 64
ink, don't dip your pen in the company's 97
ink, pen and 97
ink, spend/spill 65
jot 66
journal 67
judging a book by its cover 69
jump off the page 70
know someone like a book 18
know your Ps and Qs 101

152   BOOKISH WORDS

leaf 72
leaf, borrow/take a 72
leaf, turn down a 72
leaf, turn over a (new) 73
leaflet 73
letter, to the 112
letter of the law, the 111
lexicon 75
libel 77
line, sign on the dotted 119
lines, read between the 106
little black book 78
logo 80
lower case 138
make the headlines 58
margin 81
marginalia 82
minutes 83
miscellany 85
never judge a book by its cover 69
not a/one jot 66
not worth the paper it's written on 95
off the books 86
oldest rule in the book 23
on paper 94
on the books 86
on the same page 88
one for the book(s) 23
open book 90
orphans 144
out of sorts 92
page, bright/dark 71
page, jump off the 70

page, on the same 88
page, turn the/a new 131
page from someone's book 130
paper 93
paper, not worth the 95
paper, on/upon 94
pen 95
pen, poison 96
pen, touch the 96
pen and ink 97
pen is mightier than the sword 96
pen to paper, put/set 94
pencil 97
pencil in 98
playbook, take a page from someone's 131
poison pen 96
press, hot off the 59
press, stop (the) 129
print, fine/small 49
proof 99
Ps and Qs 101
publish 102
publish and be damned 103
pudding, proof of the 100
put pen to paper 94
read, take something as 105
read between the lines 106
read 'em and weep 105
read my lips 104
read someone a lesson/lecture 105

read someone like a book 18
read the riot act 108
read the room 104
reams 110
red-letter day 111
red-pencil 98
riot act, read the 108
royalty 112
rubber stamp 113
rubric 114
sand, written in 146
schedule 116
set pen to paper 94
shut/close the books 117
sign on the dotted line 119
singing from the same hymn sheet 89
slip 121
slush (pile) 122
small (letter), with a 146
small print 40
sorts, out of 92
speak like a book 18
speak volumes 124
spend/spill ink 65
stationer(y) 125
stereotype 127
stop (the) press 129
take a leaf out of someone's book 72
take as gospel 132

take/borrow a page from someone's book/playbook 130
take something as read 105
take the gloss off 55
taking the minutes 84
talk like a book 18
throw the book at someone 26, 134
tittle 67
trick in the book, every 18
touch the pen 96
truth, gospel 133
turn over a (new) leaf 73
turn the/a new page 131
turn-up for the books 136
typecasting 137
upper case 138
vignette 140
volumes, speak 124
watermark 142
widows 144
with a capital (letter) 145
write home about 148
write the book (on something) 19
writing 146
writing (is) on the wall 147
written all over (one's face) 148
written in sand 146
writ(ten) large/small 147